THE
FIRST
100
DAYS

A PASTOR'S GUIDE

T. SCOTT DANIELS

BEACON HILL PRESS
OF KANSAS CITY

Copyright 2011
by T. Scott Daniels and Beacon Hill Press of Kansas City

ISBN 978-0-8341-2554-4

Printed in the
United States of America

Cover Design: J.R. Caines
Interior Design: Sharon Page

Library of Congress Cataloging-in-Publication Data

Daniels, T. Scott, 1966-
  The first 100 days : a pastor's guide / T. Scott Daniels.
    p. cm.
  Includes bibliographical references (p.   ).
  ISBN 978-0-8341-2554-4 (hardcover)
 1. Pastoral theology. 2. Clergy—Appointment, call, and election.
I. Title.
  BV4011.3.D37 2011
  253'.2—dc22

2011006292

10 9 8 7 6 5 4 3 2 1

To Tharon and Barbara, my mom and dad,
who helped me get off to a great start
and modeled for me in ministry the things
that can't be taught

CONTENTS

FOREWORD

A good start is important. Sprinters spend countless hours learning how to get out of the blocks with the right technique because they know the first ten yards of a hundred-yard dash are the most important. The National Aeronautics and Space Administration tells us that if the starting projected angle for a rocket is just centimeters off at blast-off, the rocket will be wildly off target when it reaches its destination in space. Getting off to a good start definitely matters.

In the same way, every pastor knows that a good start in a new assignment is crucial. Most pastors have the luxury of a honeymoon period in a new church. While that period will vary in length, there is usually a window of "special grace" (a good Wesleyan term) offered for one to find his or her way and learn the ropes.[1] But it can also be a prime opportunity to establish different practices, offer fresh ideas, and clarify the most important priorities of the new pastor.

Dr. Scott Daniels is one of our finest pastors, preachers, and theologians. He currently pastors a great flagship church that continues to have significant influence, not only in Southern California but also for an entire denomination. Because of his creative and charismatic leadership, this historic church is reimagining a vibrant future. Much of the momentum that was created for this re-visioning came from a very good beginning.

Daniels's advice is insightful, practical, and honest. So insightful I found myself making mental notes of things I wanted to do differently; so practical I made a mental list of young pastors I wanted to share the book with; and so honest that at times I found myself shaking my head in agreement and laughing out loud.

What sets this book apart from others in a similar vein is that Daniels understands the important difference between change and transition. Several years ago, William Bridges wrote a seminal book called *Managing Transitions: Making the Most of Change.* In it, Bridges makes the case that changes are not what typically hurt an organization; it is the transitions. And changes and transitions are not the same. "*Change*," he writes, "is situational: the new site, the new boss, the new team roles, the new policy. *Transition* is the psychological process people go through to come to terms with the new situation."[2]

Most pastoral transitions are difficult because the focus is on the change, not on the transition. Thus pastors and congregations both struggle because they have not been allowed to mentally and emotionally work through the changes that most believe are necessary and would willingly embrace, if given the chance to process the transition.

I remember preparing to go to my first church as a senior pastor. I was twenty-six years old. I had been given enough information about the history of the church and the current situation by my district superintendent and a few of the board members, that I was convinced I knew in advance what changes to make. Before I even arrived, I prepared a one-page list of the "adjustments" to be made in the first year. Thankfully, I had the good sense to keep that list to myself. Instead, I spent the first two months doing a lot of listening, and I'm glad I did. I still remember the day I reached into my desk drawer and pulled out that list. I crumpled it up, put it into the trash can, and thanked God I had not shared it. It wasn't that the changes were all wrong; I just hadn't adequately calculated the transitions. Good ideas delivered at the wrong time usually end up being bad ideas.

This is not a book about change; it is a book about transition. Daniels notes, "The primary theme of this book will not be about what changes to implement in the first one hundred days of a ministry but about putting the best practices into place at the beginning of the ministry so that a pastor can quickly earn the social capital needed to make the long-term changes often necessary for transformation to take place."[3]

I believe this book is a must-read for any ministry or organizational leader, first-time pastor or seasoned veteran, who is considering a new assignment. I also believe that it will be an invaluable resource for any overseer of young pastors who would greatly benefit from the wisdom that is offered. But because this is more a book about transition than change, I would recommend *The First 100 Days* to that pastor who may not be leaving a church but is looking to help create and sustain that sacred but elusive thing called momentum.

—David A. Busic

Senior Pastor, Bethany First Church of the Nazarene

INTRODUCTION
SETTING THE RIGHT TRAJECTORY

There is an old joke about a pastor who decided one Sunday morning to call in sick, drive a couple of towns away, and play golf. The hooky-playing pastor was golfing all by himself, but unbeknownst to him two angels were looking on. One angel said to the other, "I can't believe that Reverend Johnson is skipping church in order to play golf. Somebody should do something to punish him." The second angel replied, "Watch this."

Right at that moment the minister was hitting his tee shot on a 180-yard par three. His tee shot was a horrible slice that headed directly toward the woods. The ball ricocheted off a tree and made a giant splash as it fell into a nearby creek. The first angel turned to the second and remarked, "Nice one." The second angel responded, "Just wait."

Seemingly out of nowhere a huge fish swam up the creek and grabbed the ball with its mouth and began to swim away. Then swooping down out of a tall tree, an eagle clutched the fish in its talons and took flight. The pastor could see his golf ball still protruding from the fish's mouth as the eagle flew away from him. At just the right moment, as the eagle flew directly above the green, the fish spit the ball out of its mouth causing the ball to land just above the hole. A large gust of wind came up out of nowhere causing the ball to begin to roll. The ball rolled directly toward the hole and fell into the cup. It was the most unbelievable, spectacular, and genuinely miraculous hole in one in human history.

As the pastor began to jump in the air in celebration, the first angel turned to his colleague and said, "What have you done? That guy lied to his congregation and skipped out on church this morning! Why on earth would you do that?" The second angel just grinned and replied, "Who can he tell?"

Great golf shots usually do not require that much divine intervention, but as a golfer, I have a great appreciation for all the variables that go into the perfect shot. When a great golfer makes a hole in one, all of the human aspects, including grip, swing speed, club selection, and body alignment, must be in perfect harmony. The natural aspects of distance, green speed, grass length, wind direction, temperature, and even altitude factor in as well. But I think the part of golf that makes it so challenging is *trajectory.* The face of the golf club must be in exact alignment in order for the ball to go where the player is hoping. Just turning the clubface two or three degrees to the right or left will mean the difference between a great shot and a terrible one. Every tiny degree at the tee represents ten or twenty yards of difference down the fairway. This is the basic principle of golf. If your alignment is off—even just a little bit—the results will be disastrous.

Looking around the church world today one might wonder if a great ministry tenure is as rare (and miraculous) as a hole in one in golf. Certainly there are dozens of factors that go into a successful ministry, many of which, like golf, are out of the minister's hands. But this book has been written with the conviction that if a pastor doesn't start a new ministry with great alignment, it is unlikely that the other factors will matter. What is true for golf is equally as true for ministry. If things don't get started in the right direction, they don't usually end up hitting the target. And small problems at the beginning usually lead to big problems in the end.

The concept of "the first hundred days" originated in 1933 in reference to the presidency of Franklin D. Roosevelt. In the midst of the Great Depression, FDR entered the Oval Office with a great deal of political capital as Americans were anxious for change. Working in conjunction with the Congress, President Roosevelt initiated several new programs within the first hundred days of his administration. During those first three months the president paved the way for major changes in banking, agriculture, industry, and public works. It only took FDR a hundred days to put the framework of the New Deal into place. Fairly or unfairly, the initial impact of all American presidents after him has been judged by the standard set by Roosevelt and his administration.

Although I want to borrow the time frame for this book on ministry from presidential politics, there is one major difference I want to emphasize clearly from the beginning. Whereas those who are elected president usually come into office with a great deal of momentum, authority, and political capital after waging a long, painful, and successful election campaign, pastors usually come into a new ministry position with a fair amount of goodwill from the congregation but without a whole lot of political capital to spend. Political capital—the ability to influence significant social and structural change—for a minister largely has to be earned before significant progress can be made. The primary theme of this book will not be about what changes to implement in the first one hundred days of a ministry but about putting the best practices into place at the beginning of a ministry so that a pastor can quickly earn the social capital needed to make the long-term changes often necessary for transformation to take place. So even though I want to help pastors get off to a good three-month start, the first hundred days for a minister are very different from the first hundred days given to the nation's chief executive.

Although I am a senior pastor or head of staff for a church, and this book is written largely with that role in mind, I do believe that almost all of the same prin-

ciples that apply to beginning a new tenure as a lead
pastor will apply to those who are starting various staff
and associate roles as well. It is my hope that this book
will be as helpful for pastors transitioning to their third
or fourth location of ministry as it will be for students
preparing for their first pastoral assignment.

I have tried my best to illustrate each chapter with
actual ministry stories. Some of the anecdotes are from
my own ministry or the pastoral experiences of my
family. Many of the stories are from friends who have
been willing to share with me some of their wisdom and
experience. Although all of the stories are true, in nearly
every case I have changed the names, locations, and a
few of the details so that no one will be hurt. If some of
the stories sound familiar, it is likely that this is because
pastors often make the same mistakes and there really
is "nothing new under the sun." In some places I admit
to some of my own successes and failures. In the stories that are mine I have changed the names not for my
protection but out of care for those I've served as pastor.
Although I believe I have a pretty decent track record of

starting ministries well, I have learned far more from my mistakes than I have from my successes.

Beyond personal experience and interviews with other pastors, much of the research for this book has come from exploring other ministry authors and from business books about how CEOs can get off to a good start. I am keenly aware—and make it a habit to say often—that leading a congregation is *very* different from running a business, but I do think there are some principles that great CEOs have used to get off to a good leadership start that apply well to ministry. I have read several of these kinds of works in preparation for writing this text, and I am grateful for much of what I have gleaned there.

Leading the body of Christ in extending the mission of the kingdom of Christ in the world is the most significant work a person can take on. I am convinced that far too often today great and vital locations for ministry implode unnecessarily, leaving local churches (and thus the kingdom) severely damaged in their wake. My hope is that helping ministers get aligned correctly will help men and women have more successful ministries over the long haul. If we can start with the right alignment, who knows where, with God's help, our ministries might lead?

ON YOUR MARK, GET SET, REFLECT

Let me begin this book about getting off to a good start in a new ministry with three of my favorite sayings from the ancient philosopher Socrates. Socrates says,

- "The unexamined life is not worth living."[4]
- "Life contains but two tragedies. One is not to get your heart's desire; the other is to get it."[5]
- "Know thyself."[6]

If you have picked up this book, chances are you are just finishing your preparation for ministry and you are getting ready to start your first ministry position, you are considering making a move to a new ministry, you are in the midst of a transition to a new location of ministry, or you have just made the big move and you are already looking for help. If you have already moved or have already made the decision to move, you can probably skip to the second chapter, but if you are just starting out in ministry or contemplating a transition, I want to give you some things to consider as you pray for God's guidance.

First, the Unexamined Life Is Not Worth Living

One of my favorite Old Testament stories is the calling of the boy Samuel in 1 Sam. 3. The first three times the Lord called out to Samuel, he ran to the priest Eli convinced it was he who had called out to him in the night. But finally, with Eli's help, Samuel was able to discern that it was the voice of the Lord calling to him and not Eli or even his own imagination. Correctly discerning the voice of God is a tricky thing. One of the

[handwritten margin notes: "Samuel needed help discerning", "Eli's help", "God's call"]

most challenging aspects of being human is our amazing ability for self-deception. Especially in the church where our conversations are often wrapped in God language, it is easy as a pastor to claim God is calling us to a transition when in reality it is our family who wants to move. We say it's God's will, but it is really the desire to escape a contentious board member at our current assignment. We say it is God's leading, but it's really the tug of our own ego. Isn't it amazing how often God's leading also includes a significant salary increase?

It's not that family pressures, emotional exhaustion, or even financial needs aren't legitimate issues and may even be part of the reason why God might lead a pastor to a new place of ministry or why a first-time minister might consider one opportunity over another. There are literally hundreds of factors to consider when one seeks God's wisdom about a ministry move. The point I want to make is simply this, take the time necessary to prayerfully examine and explore the reasons why you are considering a ministry transition or why you are thinking about a move to a new ministry or a new location.

I grew up in a family full of ministers. When I was young, my father made several ministry transitions. By the time I was thirteen, we had lived in thirteen different homes and my dad had served as a pastor in eight different churches. Needless to say, I was used to making transitions. Thankfully, my parents stayed in their eighth ministry assignment for almost twenty years, but I was at home with them only for the first five before heading off to college.

I have now been in ministry for twenty-five years, and here is what I have discovered about myself. After about three years in one location I start to get antsy. It is as though an internal alarm clock goes off somewhere deep inside me and a voice from within says, "Okay, Scott, isn't it about time to move? I think you are ready for the next adventure! It's probably time for us to start moving on . . ." I have listened to and obeyed that internal voice several times. And even when I haven't obeyed that voice, I have had strong arguments with it. Sometimes I have named that voice as the voice of God. It may have been. But it also may have just been my life-long habit of transitioning to a new location every three or four years, pushing me to make moves that may or may not have been in God's wisdom and will for me.

It took some time for me to figure out what was going on. My wife, some good friends, and even some good counselors have helped me to see what I could not. God has helped me recognize all kinds of reasons why I have a tendency to live waiting for the next big opportunity. These discoveries about myself are helping me to be happier and more content where I am and with what God is doing in the location he has me in right now. Most importantly he is helping me become a better finisher. One of the things moving frequently helped me to become was a good starter. (It is part of the reason I can write this book.) But to this day, I have yet to experience the joy of being a good finisher. I'm hoping that is what God is helping me to become now.

The point is not to try and talk you out of the ministry transition you sense God may be calling you to make at this moment. The point here at the start is simply to encourage you to take time to examine your life, your motives, and where God is working. "The unexamined life is not worth living," and the unexamined ministry is a recipe for disaster. Before you make any ministry transition, take time to pray, listen, and ensure you know it is God who is leading you and calling you to a new location, a new ministry, and a new adventure with him.

Second, Life Contains but Two Tragedies—One Is Not to Get Your Heart's Desire; the Other Is to Get It

I love to ask fellow pastors about their ministry careers. This is anecdotal, but I have often found it to be the case that when ministers who are retired or near retirement reflect over their pastoral careers, they look back at one location of ministry as "the one that got away." Here are three examples from recent conversations I have had with pastor friends.

When I look back over my ministry career, I realize that I made a mistake leaving First Church when I did. I was young. The church was growing rapidly. I began to feel like I was in over my head. We had outgrown the building we were in, and I wasn't sure what to do next. What I needed to do was ask for a six-week sabbatical to go visit two or three churches that were doing ministry at the next level up and learn from them. Instead I got overwhelmed and tired and when an interesting opportunity came along, I took it. God has redeemed that hasty decision. But looking back I realize I left before I should have.

///////////////////////////////////////

I think of the years we spent at the Riverside Church as the pinnacle years of our ministry. Our kids grew up while we were there. The church loved us as a family, and the ministry was really thriving. But one day I got a call telling me that I was being offered a significant administrative role in the denomination. I was raised to respect authority, and here I was with an authority on the phone asking me to move. As I look back now, I realize I was doing more to help the denomination while I was leading that church than I ever did in that administrative role. What I needed at the time was the courage to say no, but I didn't have it.

///////////////////////////////////////

My greatest regret looking back is leaving Main Street Church when we did. We had taken the church from almost nothing to a very significant congregation. But then I got a call from a bigger church with a better salary. What I soon discovered was it had bigger problems. So I left a church where I was loved and went to a church that nearly killed me. Looking back I should have been honest with the church leadership about my financial needs and about the need for the church to learn with me how to operate at the next level of leadership and administrative structure. Instead of helping them move ahead I took an easy exit and it damaged both the church and my family in the long run.

Again, my goal is not to get you to change your mind about making a transition but to encourage you to take the time needed to reflect and pray. It takes time and most likely the input of a few Elis in our lives to learn to hear God's voice clearly. We also need to heed Socrates' most famous piece of advice.

Third, Know Thyself

I have a theory that there are four categories of ministers. There are activators, rebuilders, sustainers, and maximizers.

Activators are those leaders with the strengths necessary to create something out of nothing. They are great at church planting. They are able to go into an existing congregation and create a youth ministry where there has never been one or launch a music ministry where no one has ever done more than pick a couple of hymns to sing. Like God, who created ex nihilo (out of nothing), activators are driven and have the qualities necessary to start new ministries.

Rebuilders are those ministers who read Ezra and Nehemiah and get inspired. Like those two great leaders who directed the people of Judah in the reconstruction of Jerusalem's worship and walls, rebuilders have the ability to go into a ministry situation that many, if not most, have written off as hopeless and bring new life to it. Rebuilders thrive on and have the strengths to put the pieces of a broken ministry or church back together.

It is a unique leader who can come into a ministry that is growing and vibrant and keep it moving forward. *Sustainers* Sustainers have the wisdom and sensitivity to enter into a healthy church or ministry and not mess things up. Like Samuel, sustainers have the heart of a priest, and they know how to love others and keep people united even through transitions in leadership.

✱ Maximizers are those leaders who look for situations that are healthy but are ready to explode and move far beyond where they are right now. Maximizers have the ability to motivate people to follow a big vision, and they are self-assured enough in their own strengths to willingly surround themselves with the people capable of bringing that big vision to life.

It is my theory that most ministers fall quite naturally into one, or maybe two, of those four categories. Most of us are by nature activators, rebuilders, sustainers, or maximizers.

Not long ago my wife remarked to me, "Have you noticed that we have had a knack for leading very broken ministries?" I don't think she meant that we have a gift for breaking healthy ministries, but I think she meant that in most of our twenty years together we have partnered in ministries that were rebuilding projects of one kind or another. She was right. With just one or maybe two exceptions, my ministry has been about entering into a fairly broken or damaged ministry location and bringing health to it. What was interesting about her comment was not just how insightful it was, but that it was in the context of how much we actually enjoy being part of rebuilding ministries.

As I have come to "know myself," I have come to realize that God has gifted me in ways that make me a strong rebuilder or a maximizer. And because of that, my most gratifying opportunities of ministry have been where I've been able to put those strengths to work.

I love to hear stories about people who moved into a neighborhood and planted a church and their ministry took off and is doing amazing things. I am so deeply envious of activators. It is truly a gift to have the ability to start something from nothing. However, I know I do not have that gift, nor do I have that temperament. I am just introverted enough to fail miserably as an activator.

I am a huge fan of author Jan Karon's Mitford novels. Karon's books are about Father Tim's experiences as a pastor in the quaint small town of Mitford. The stories are delightful, beautiful, and profound. Father Tim lives the sacred priestly life of the sustainer in the Mayberryesque community of Mitford. I am drawn to these books because I am drawn to the powerful integrity and profound simplicity of the sustaining ministry of Father Tim. Although I currently live in one of the world's largest cities, if I received a call from Mitford First Church on just the right Monday, I might just be tired enough to take it. But I know in my heart that I would last about nine months in Mitford before the maximizer in me would go insane. I can't tell you how much I wish I had the strengths of the sustainer. I think pastors whom God has given the gifts of a sustainer are truly the salt of the earth. But I simply do not have the strengths or temperament of a sustainer. It's not how God formed me.

That is simply my point: "Know thyself." Try to figure out how God has gifted you, and reflect over what may be the right fit for you given your strengths, passion, and temperament. There are many temperament and strengths assessment tools available these days to assist you in this process. One that I have found particularly helpful is the StrengthsQuest materials sponsored by the Gallup organization.[7]

It is also important to understand the right cultural fit. There are multiple aspects to culture, far more than I could list here. No matter where you transition, there will be aspects of a new culture or setting that you will have to learn and adjust to. But there are deeply rooted cultural preferences within each of us that we ought to be aware of. When pastoral tenures fail rapidly, these are the kinds of comments I often hear:

- "She was an East Coaster at heart, and she never understood the laid-back West."

- "Pastor Hall never quite adjusted to being part of a 'professional' church. I'm not sure he even owned a suit."

- "I think Rev. Miller wanted to spend his time with young people, and we just are not that youthful of a church."

- "Pastor Wright just kept talking about the way they used to do ministry in Chicago. But we aren't like the big city, and we don't want to be."
- "She was too academic, and we're just simple folk."
- "He was so simplistic, and we're in a thoughtful, educated college town."
- "I don't think he could ever get over the reality that we were never going to raise our hands in worship."

Rural or urban, conservative or progressive, professional or casual, diverse or homogeneous, scholarly or practical, youthful or multigenerational—these are just scratching the surface of the different cultures a church embodies. And it is important for a leader to understand what kind of cultural fit works best for him or her.

It took twenty-five years for me to recognize that I am most invigorated when I get to do ministry in a highly secular community. Although there is much that I love (and miss) about living and working in what is often referred to as the Bible Belt, I know enough about myself now to know that I prefer doing ministry in a setting where it is a challenge to be a Christian and where churches of various denominations are forced to work together instead of competing with one another. For some, the huge cultural challenges and the often slow growth of secular urban settings would be overwhelming. For me it is energizing. That doesn't make one temperament bad and another one good. It is simply the product of nurture and nature. And I believe it is important to think seriously about cultural fit before making a transition.

So take this initial advice as a word from the wise Socrates: "Know thyself."

KNOW
WHAT YOU
DON'T KNOW

There is a legendary story about a new young Method-
ist minister who moved to Georgia fresh out of seminary to pastor his first church. He felt fully prepared
for ministry and was excited to make a huge difference
in the world. As soon as he pulled into town, he drove
directly to the church to get a look at his new parish. He
was awed by the quaint beauty of the old church that
was rich in history yet looked so warm and inviting.
However, one of the first things the new pastor noticed
was a gnarled old tree that blocked the side doors of the

church building. He frowned to himself and thought, "That tree is a terrible eyesore and a serious fire hazard. I can't believe that no one has done anything about it?" And so he decided in that moment that a great way to show his new congregation his youthful energy and decisive leadership skills would be to take care of this obvious problem himself and cut down the tree as a gracious surprise for the church members before his first Sunday morning. And so he proceeded to cut down the tree.

The young pastor's well-intentioned decision came with both good news and bad news. The bad news was that he had not realized that the tree was believed by the congregation to have been planted by John Wesley—the founder of Methodism—hundreds of years earlier while he was a missionary in Georgia. The good news was that the new pastor did not have to go through the bother of unpacking all of his boxes. His tenure as pastor was over before he got to his first Sunday.[8]

The first step in a ministry transition is to know who you are. The second step is to know (as best you can) where you are going and what you are getting yourself into. As you transition to a new ministry setting, beginning on day one, there are three factors to constantly be aware of: the church's past, the church's present, and the church's context.

Become a Historian

It is unfortunate, but many pastors entering into new ministry settings fail to become historians and ignore, to their own demise, the past patterns of a congregation. No two churches are alike. All congregations have unique histories, customs, communication patterns, traditions, leadership models, and expectations of a pastor. A church is a unique culture, and the one who is called to lead that culture must understand its history well.

There are two metaphors I have found very helpful on this point. One is from a fellow pastor, and the other is from the Scriptures. Pastor John Galloway argues that ministers should think of themselves as people invited to be facilitators at someone else's family reunion. New pastors should consider themselves as the ones invited to attend and coordinate the reunion, but they aren't

family (yet). Galloway imagines himself as the facilitator at the Smythe family reunion, writing,

> As we will no doubt discover in our first fifteen
> minutes glad-handing under the tent, each family
> possesses its own personality, its own history, its
> own touchy points, its own well-established ways
> of being family and running reunions. The Smythes
> have been at it for years, and their habits are set
> in stone. So we are arriving to pick up the ongoing
> enterprise of people we really do not know, in a fa-
> cility we do not recognize, to lead them at a reunion
> whose activities they have already been practicing
> for years quite well without us, thank you, with
> well-cultivated idiosyncrasies we have never seen
> in our lives. In an assignment that might be called
> "mission impossible," they look to us to lead. To
> complicate our assignment, they will for a period
> of time accept our leadership, but only insofar as it
> reinforces the Smythe way of doing things, a way
> they refuse to make clear to us until we violate it
> and incur their scorn. . . . We are the facilitators at
> an extended family reunion in a family to which we

do not belong, who have a well-developed style we have never seen, in a place we do not recognize.[9]

I love Pastor Galloway's metaphor. Too often new pastors make the mistake of believing they are in charge immediately, when time and knowledge are required to earn the credibility necessary for leadership. Credibility, authority, and permission to lead come with time, but they will not come at all without quickly developing a thorough understanding of and a deep appreciation for the history and traditions of this new church family.

A second metaphor I find helpful comes from the last book in the New Testament. A few years ago I became fascinated with the seven letters written to the churches in Rev. 2–3. What interested me most was that each of the letters is addressed to the "angel" of the church. I wanted to know why these letters of both judgment and encouragement from the Lord were not written directly to the Asian congregations but to their "angels." After doing a great deal of research I came to the conclusion that,

> John the Revelator writes to the angels of the
> churches because he recognizes something profound

and complex about the way churches are formed as communities. The seven churches of Asia—like all communal bodies—are more than the sum of the individuals that make up that community. Communities, like the individual persons from which they are formed, take on a kind of spirit, personality, or "life of their own" that becomes greater than the sum of their physical parts. The seven angels of the churches, to whom John writes, are neither disconnected spiritual beings nor merely a colorful way of describing nonexistent realities. Instead, the term "angel" signifies the very real ethos or communal essence that either gives life to or works at destroying the fabric of the very community that gave birth to it.[10]

In other words, I think John addresses the angel of each of the churches because he recognizes that there is an ethos, culture, or history that shapes every congregation. The collective culture of a church can be helpful or hurtful. (In the case of the seven letters, five of those seven "angels" were not helpful to the mission of Christ.) But regardless of whether or not the culture formed by the history of a congregation brings life or dysfunction, the opportunity to change the congregation begins with the ability to understand the nature of the angel of that particular church. I am convinced that a pastor cannot hope to really bring about transformation in a new location of ministry until he or she has come to know the angel of the church he or she has been called to lead. And the only way to get to know the ethos, culture, spirit, or "angel" of a congregation is to discover its history.

What are the best ways to discover the history of a church? Certainly some of the background information about the church was covered in the interview process. But more often than not, interviewing is like the early weeks of a dating relationship. While dating, both parties are putting forward their best selves for the other and trying as best they can to hide the negative parts of who they are. It is important that you ask probing and insightful questions in an interview process, but even the best interviewers and interviewees will fail to learn enough about the church's historical context to lead well. There just simply isn't enough time in the interview process to learn everything you need to know.

Like the unexpected discoveries spouses make about one another in the first years of marriage, on every one of the first one hundred days, a new pastor will learn something he or she did not know about the people he or she is now called upon to shepherd. So here are some important things to discover during the first hundred days on the job.

Pay attention to the rate of turnover of the previous pastors. Are there any patterns you notice about the tenures of those who came before you? Did the previous pastors leave well or leave poorly? Did they go on to healthy ministries or did they leave damaged and broken? If previous pastors have tended to have long tenures and have left in healthy ways, try to discover some of the things they did well that helped them to be successful. If on the other hand, the pastors before you left damaged and broken, try to discover what dysfunctions they exhibited, the congregation exhibited, or both, and work at forming new patterns.

Be careful, however, as you explore the tenures of the pastors who came before you. When people want to talk to you about what previous pastors did well and not so well, listen but don't say very much in response. Remember there are always two sides to every story, and so avoid taking sides and refrain from the temptation to temporarily make yourself look and feel better by holding yourself up as better in contrast to your predecessors. Also remember that people who seem to enjoy being critical of the previous three pastors will more than likely get great joy out of being critical about you in the not-so-distant future.

In some cases you may be entering an extremely damaged situation where the previous pastor had to leave because of marital infidelity or some other form of broken trust. Even though some in the congregation will be extremely angry and hurt at the previous leader, it is critical that you stay above those emotions and not demonize your predecessor. Help the church heal by treating your predecessor with the grace you would want extended to you if you were in the same situation.

I think it is very valuable to know as much as you can about the tenures of those who came before you. Those who do not know their history are doomed to repeat it. But great leaders are always big people; not necessarily in stature or even in giftedness, but in character. People of small character have a need to succeed at the expense of others. Leaders with big character are able to celebrate the great things done by those who have gone before them (and of those still around them) and build upon those victories.

Joshua had the self-assurance and courage to follow Israel's first great prophet and most powerful deliverer without having to tear down the leadership legacy of Moses in the process. He led the people of Israel into the Promised Land standing on the shoulders of Moses by using the gifts God had uniquely given to him.

David inherited the throne from a king so broken he was literally coming apart psychologically. But David refused to make the foundation of his leadership the broken reputation of Saul. David's depth of character was demonstrated in his unwillingness to lay a hand on the "Lord's anointed" (see 1 Sam. 24:6). For a good lesson in what happens to those who build their future on the demise of others, read the story of Absalom in 2 Sam. 13–18—he tries to become king by destroying the character of his father, David.

If it is a comfortable and appropriate situation, I would encourage you to talk to one or more of the previous pastors about their tenure at the church. It is sometimes considered inappropriate to talk to a previous pastor while the interview process is going on (not always, but sometimes). But once the decision has been made and you are in the first one hundred days in your new ministry, I think it is appropriate to write a letter to the previous pastor or pastors to thank them for their leadership in that location of ministry and ask them to pray for you that God would help you build upon the foundation Christ helped them to establish. I would then follow up with a phone call—if appropriate—a few weeks later to talk with them and get their perspective on the church and its history.

If you are entering into a lead pastor role, another suggestion for discovering a church's history is to take the time to read through the board minutes from the year or two prior to your arrival. Although the minutes from meetings can be somewhat sanitary compared to some of the actual debates themselves, it is often very helpful to get some idea of what issues have been considered important by the leadership board in the past. The minutes frequently reveal what topics are touchy and could be potential land mines in the future. And board minutes can often help one know quickly who some of the primary influencers are and which direction those leaders tend to move the conversation (forward or backward).

Lawrence Farris suggests that when a pastor enters a new ministry, he or she should have a congregational history-telling event in conjunction with a church supper. He even suggests that a good way to structure the dinner is "to have people seated for the meal according to their presence during various pastorates. As people eat, they are asked to share what some of the congregational accomplishments were during that pastorate, and to recall what some of the challenges were."[11]

I think that is a wonderful idea. Reverend Earl Darden, who was a great mentor to me in my first pastorate and who has now gone to heaven, once told me the first six months at a new church he would recommend that a new pastor go to lunch with all the current church board members and as many of the key lay leaders as he could in order to ask each of them the same set of three questions. He even suggested that the new pastor bring a notebook to write down and keep track of their answers. The three questions he suggested were:

1. What are your two or three most memorable moments as you have been part of this church or ministry? Or what do you consider the glory days of this church?

2. What is your favorite thing about this church or ministry? Or what is the one thing about this church or ministry that you would hope no one would ever change?

3. And if you had one dream for this church or ministry, what would it be?

No matter what approach you take in becoming a historian of the church or ministry you have now been called to lead, have as many conversations as you can about its history. If for no other reason, conversations about a church's history show people you care about them and about who they are as a community. Remember, you are the facilitator at another family's reunion. You will not lead the family forward, and you will certainly not be considered for adoption into the family, until you care enough to know the family history well.

Assess the Present

I spent a lot of paragraphs encouraging you to learn the church's history because I am so convinced that it is an area where so many pastors fail, and fail quickly. But it is also important that you assess where the church or ministry is in the present. Three areas about the present that are critical to get a handle on in the first hundred days are the church's mission, the shape of the finances, and the state of paid and lay leadership.

Pastor Gene came to Hillside Church with a mission statement in mind that had functioned very well in his previous ministry location. He believed in it so deeply that he had planned during his first ten-week sermon series at Hillside to repeat the powerful series he had used at his previous church on various aspects of the new mission statement so that it would quickly become embraced and engrained by the people of Hillside. But the very first week he revealed the new mission statement and proceeded to preach on its kingdom significance, he started to meet with strong resistance from the people. He quickly learned that Hillside already had a mission statement. It was a mission statement that had been developed over a great deal of time with the previous pastor and had involved all kinds of special committee meetings to get the wording just right. Several new ministries were started in the church to put the church's mission statement into practice. One parishioner even pointed out that the church's mission statement was painted on the fellowship hall wall. (Pastor Gene hadn't even noticed it or made that connection yet.) Pastor Gene quickly started working on a different sermon series.

If a church's vision has been formalized in mission statements and in various ministries, usually this will come up in an interview. But many times what is viewed by the congregation as the primary vision or purpose of the church is not found in formal mission statements but in the informal practices of the church, and this latent vision takes time to be revealed. It is vitally important that a pastor quickly come to understand what mission the church already envisions itself living out before altering that mission significantly. Here are some mission-related questions worth getting a handle on:

- What do the people consider to be the church's greatest strength?
- What impact does the church have currently on the community?
- What role does the church see the pastor fulfilling?
- What would the people say makes the church unique or different from the other churches in the area?
- Is there a special emphasis in one ministry area such as evangelism, worship, discipleship, or service?

Pastor Lisa had done an amazing job as youth minister at Avondale church, a small-town church in the Southeast. The number of teens in the church had increased significantly, but most impressively she had put together an amazing mission program that had young people involved in ministry in the community and all over the world. She had rightly received a great deal of attention regionally for the work she was doing, and so predictably she soon received a call from First Church, a much larger church in the city with youth facilities she could only dream about at a country church like Avondale. She prayed about the decision to make the move, but she didn't have to pray very long. There were so many more teens to reach in the city, and the thought of what God could help her accomplish in the lives of young people in a church with first-rate facilities was too exciting to pass up.

But when she got to First Church, she realized that although her salary had increased and her responsibilities had grown exponentially, her youth ministry budget was less than half the size at First Church as it had been at Avondale. Because Avondale was an old church, it had no mortgage, and because its staff was small, it didn't spend a high percentage of its income on salaries. Therefore, it was able to invest a good deal of money, for a church its size, in ministry and missions in particular. First Church, on the other hand, was still paying (and paying significantly) for the mortgage that came with their first-class facility. It needed a larger staff and the cost of living in the city was much higher; over half of the church's income went toward staff salaries and benefits. This meant that ministries had to operate on a shoestring. Lisa wasn't sure what to do. She was used to building ministry for youth on mission opportunities, but missions cost money, and her new ministry had very little of that to go around.

It is critical for a pastor to figure out the current state of the church's finances within the first one hundred days. Especially if you are in a lead pastor role, learn immediately not only how much the church has but also its debt load, its giving history, and its weekly financial procedures. You will have to decide whether or not you will have access to the giving records of individuals in the church. There are good arguments for both knowing and not knowing that information. Some pastors do not want to know what individuals give because they believe their lack of knowledge helps them to treat everyone graciously without having a conscious or subconscious financial bias. Other pastors think that they need to know this information because they can treat people equally despite their giving record but that giving information is too important not to have when making decisions about leadership, budget planning, and so on. Either way, it is critical to find out who has access to that information, who are the individuals able to sign checks, and how congregational budgeting is done. It is easy to fail in the area of finances. So understand the state of the church financially, who controls the finances, and how the budgeting process works before the first hundred days are over.

Get to know the leadership team of the church or ministry as quickly as possible. Invest time getting to know them and their families. In a small church, lay leaders are critical to the success of a minister. I would suggest that you not make significant leadership changes in the first three to six months. A pastor who I consider to be a great model once told me, "Son, in the first two years at a new church preach well and don't change anything except your underwear." That may be quaint, but there is wisdom there. I am always amazed in the fourth or fifth year of a ministry at how many people I thought were leaders when I first arrived at the church ended up not being good leaders and how many people I didn't even know (or who weren't even at the church four years ago) are the most significant leaders now.

If you are a pastor moving to a larger church that has some pastoral staff in place, I think the same rules largely apply with paid leadership as with lay leadership. It is my suggestion that you make decisions that involve personnel transitions slowly. Take time to get to know the pastoral staff well and for them to get to know you. There may ultimately be some difficult personnel decisions to make, but I have been amazed at how many times staff people recognize that they are not a good fit with a new leader and end up making a move of their own accord.

I think the language the church uses regarding not only lead pastors but also staff pastors is important. No pastor is ever *hired* for ministry. They are *called* into a ministry position. This is a critical distinction. In the business world people are hired to do a job. Therefore, even though it is not easy in the world of business to fire someone, it is done with some regularity and it is usually accomplished with little residual effect to the company that let the person go. But in the church, a pastor is *called* because he or she is not just doing a job; he or she is being invited to enter a community. I believe this is why the often necessary transitions of personnel in a church are so difficult. The church and you as its leader are not just asking an employee to leave but intentionally eliminating someone from the community. I cannot emphasize this enough. Make personnel and leadership changes slowly, carefully, and with great grace.

Learn About the Community

Finally, get to know the context or community surrounding the ministry or church. Especially if you have moved to a part of the country with which you are not familiar, get to know the community. Robert Ramey suggests several aspects of a new community that a pastor ought to begin mapping out in his or her mind from the start. Here are some of his suggestions:

1. Make a membership map. Figure out what part of the community most of your members live in, work in, and participate in.

2. Make an evangelism map. Learn where target outreach communities are that surround the church.

3. Make a boundary map. What are the natural boundaries that limit the reach of this particular local church?

4. Create a populations-and-lifestyle map. What kind of people live in the communities that form the church's evangelism map and what are their primary needs?

5. Make a centers-of-community map. Get to know the name of the key streets, shopping malls, schools, libraries, and other churches in the area.

6. Make a major-institutions map. Discover the primary employers, educational institutions, hospitals, military bases, and prisons that are nearby.[12]

There is more important historical, contemporary, and contextual information about a new ministry than can possibly be learned in the first one hundred days. But if a new pastor can become a historian, a student of the current situation, and an observer of the surrounding environment, he or she is well on the way to getting a ministry heading in the right direction.

HELP
YOUR
FAMILY
TRANSITION

When I shared with my wife, Debbie, what I thought the chapters of this book would most likely be, there were two she snickered at. She giggled at the last chapter on self-care and at this chapter on helping your family make the transition. Her laugh was not a good laugh. It was a snicker that implied I might want to find an outside author to write these two chapters. I will admit that I am writing both these chapters mainly on the basis of what other authors suggest and from the experience of my own failures. Although I am fairly certain that every member of my family is currently very happy, I have without a doubt put my children through at least two very tough transitions and my wife through at least four. (I'll come back to self-care, but that has been a challenge for me also.)

Nevertheless, despite my own shortcomings in this particular area, let me emphasize that one of your highest priorities in the first hundred days of transition ought to be to take care of your family. Their needs in transition should be one of your primary concerns. I would agree wholeheartedly with Robert Ramey's observation that "if I had to do it over again, I would spend more time at home, unpacking the china, taking my children to school, and doing little chores that would have eased all of us into a new situation."[13] Besides spending as much time as possible with your family during a transition, let me suggest three ways to help make your household relocation easier on the entire family. First, as much as possible, involve the whole family in the decision-making process. Second, take some time for a transition break in between ministry assignments. And third, work hard at making sure your family feels plugged in as quickly as possible into the new community.

Discerning God's Direction as a Family

This is one area where we actually have done fairly well as a family. If you have a spouse, obviously any transition in ministry will intimately involve him or her. As a lead pastor, I will not interview a staff-pastor candidate without including his or her spouse in the process. This is not just for the sake of knowing what that spouse is like (although that is significant), but more importantly it is to make sure that the spouse is included in the decision process and is fully aware of all that is involved in the potential transition to a new location of ministry.

There may be circumstances where it is a huge challenge financially for the interviewing church to include both pastor and spouse in the interview process. But personally, despite the economic challenges, I would refuse to accept any call to ministry if Debbie had not been part of the interview and decision-making process.

As I wrote in the last chapter, people are not hired into ministry, they are called into it. That call includes an invitation to become a significant part of a community. Because it is a call to bind our lives together in the body of Christ, I think it is unfair for a spouse not to be included in the process. Not only do I need Debbie's insights and intuitions, but I also need her support and partnership in such a significant major life transition.

I would encourage you, however, to also include your children in the process. They obviously don't need to be part of the interview, but at least the children in your household who are old enough to understand (and to keep confidences) should be included in family prayer and conversation about the decision.

As Debbie and I were preparing to interview in Pasadena, California, where we are now, we began to talk with our two oldest sons—who were twelve and nine at the time—about the possibilities of God leading us from Texas to California. We were especially concerned about our oldest son, Caleb, who had good friends at our former church, liked his school a great deal, and has a personality that generally prefers familiar routines to radically new ones. In fact we were worried enough about him making the transition well, that had he been highly resistant to moving, he may have rightly been the deciding factor in staying or going. But one night, just before Debbie and I flew out to California to interview, Debbie was sitting in bed reading her Bible and journaling when Caleb came walking in and sat down next to her on the bed. It was obvious that he wanted to talk about something. Finally, he said to her, "Mom, I've been thinking. If God wants us to go to California, it will be hard, but we have to go."

We were certainly shocked, blessed, and thankful for Caleb's childlike trust in God's purposes. And we were grateful that we had included him in at least some of the conversations, because his confirmation of trust in God gave his mother and me the freedom to go to California for the interview with hearts and minds open to God's leading. The decision to respond to a new call of God impacts the whole family, and so, if it is possible, I believe it is wise to include all of the family in the prayerful consideration of any major transition.

Take Time to Transition

One thing I have failed to do in my last two ministry relocations is to leave enough time between ministry assignments to transition the family well. If I had it to do over again, I would do it differently.

In August of 2002 I received a call from Richardson Church of the Nazarene (just outside of Dallas) to become their senior pastor. At the time I was a professor of theology and ethics at Southern Nazarene University (SNU) near Oklahoma City. I had taught there for six years and was doing some pulpit supply for Richardson during the summer when they suggested I just stay on and become their permanent pastor. It genuinely felt like the moving of God's Spirit as all of the pieces came together and a call to pastor the church was extended to our family at the end of the summer.

I was extremely excited to make the transition to the church, but I had already signed a teaching contract for the 2002-3 school year with SNU. Although it would have been a challenge for the university to fill my classes with different professors so close to the start of school, they probably could have done it. Although Richardson more than likely would have waited for me to start as their full-time pastor until after the end of first semester (thus giving SNU time to fill my position), I was too excited about getting started to ask the church to wait until December or January. So instead, I moved Debbie and our four very young children to Dallas in August so the older kids could start school, and I commuted back and forth for sixteen weeks until the first semester was over. I would stay with my parents in Oklahoma City and teach classes Monday through Thursday, and then I would drive down to Dallas and be with my family and the church Friday through Sunday.

In hindsight, it was a poor and likely unnecessary decision, and it was very hard on my wife and kids. The low moment during those four months for my wife and me was one afternoon when Debbie called me from Dallas to tell me that she had picked up Caleb from his new school and that he had obviously been crying. She asked him how his day had gone and who he had played with at recess. He told her that he didn't do anything good and that at recess he went out to the big map of the United States painted on the playground blacktop and just sat down on Oklahoma and cried throughout the break period. Either way it may have been a tough transition for him, but I should have been there also to take him out for ice cream or throw the baseball around or to sit on Oklahoma and cry with him.

Unfortunately, I didn't really learn my lesson and we did a very similar thing—only this time in reverse—when we moved to Pasadena in 2006. Pasadena First called us in February of that year, and we decided I would begin my work as pastor of the church in early April. Debbie and the kids came out with me for the first two Sundays, but then they went back to Dallas for about eight weeks so the kids could finish up school and we could try and sell our house. Pasadena First had an excellent interim pastor, and although they were anxious for me to start, they could have easily waited until June for us to come as a family. But I was again excited about starting, and it is hard to stay anywhere once a decision has been made to move. It was not only a very lonely seven or eight weeks for me in California but more importantly a huge burden on Debbie to try and deal with four kids all alone while also trying to get the house ready for the movers to come. It was too much stress on her, and looking back now, what seemed so urgent at the time could have happened with much less tension, anxiety, and family trauma. No transition is ever easy, but take my advice built on hard knocks: Relax. Take a long view of the situation and figure out how to take the time your family needs to minimize the strain of the transition for them.

Roy Oswald, in his book *New Beginnings,* shares about a pastor who always insisted on having a one-month interim between pastoral assignments:

> We had a lot of things to talk about—what it was like saying goodbye to the congregation—what our stay there had meant to us—some of the hopes and dreams that had to be let go. We also discussed the future as a family in a new place—what things we wanted to do differently this time—what things would be important for us to continue as a family. The month went very quickly. When it was over, we were ready to begin ministry in the new parish.[14]

Speaking from negative experience, I would strongly encourage you to give yourself this kind of space if possible as you move from one ministry assignment to another.

I have come to the place personally where I would recommend this interim time in almost every situation. But in particular if you are leaving a ministry context where you were bruised, battered, and damaged, I would almost deem it mandatory. It is not an unusual situation today for a pastor to leave a ministry setting not by choice but due to pressure from the congregation to leave. When a pastor is asked to leave a church, the whole family, and not just the pastor, carries the pain of that sense of loss and brokenness. It is unrealistic to believe that a wounded pastor and family can move quickly from a place of hurt and damage immediately into another context of ministry without taking some time to heal together. In the long run, your new church desperately needs your family to succeed, and this is one way to make sure the first hundred days and beyond go well for the family.

Helping the Family Connect

One additional challenge for the family is the different speeds at which family members get plugged into a new community and into a new culture. Often the pastor doesn't sense this because he or she is immediately immersed into dozens of relationships at the church, and so relationally the transition happens rapidly for him or her. But the children who may or may not be in school and the spouse who may or may not be plugged into work can easily feel lonely and left out while the pastor feels not only connected but also already oversaturated with relationships.

Find ways to begin connecting your family in relationship with people at the church. When we were finally all together as a family in Richardson, the church set up one dinner party a week for the first several weeks with various groups in the church. It was a nice way for us to get to know a good percentage of the church members in a short period of time. But at every party they would make sure at least one family was invited who had children around the same age as ours. I think one family in particular, the Thomases, ended up being asked to go to over half of these initial get-togethers so that our children would have someone they knew to play and connect with. It was a very kind thing for their family to be willing to attend as many parties as they did. It took us three or four of these dinner events before it dawned on us what the Thomas family had committed to do. We still tease them that they were our "stalker family" because it seemed like everywhere we went, they were there too. But inviting families with kids the same age as ours to attend those early social gatherings was a wonderful idea and an extremely kind thing to do. It helped our kids survive and get connected.

I think it is also important to subscribe, at least for the first few months, to the local newspaper if for no other reason than to discover there the fun things to do in the surrounding area. Once we were all together in Southern California, we designated Fridays as family time and looked for something fun in the area to do every week. One Friday we went to the beach; the next Friday we went to a Dodger game. One Friday we rode the train to downtown and attended an outdoor concert;

the next Friday we drove to Beverly Hills and walked down Rodeo Drive. The church was very kind and gave our family tickets to Disneyland as a welcome gift. We saved some money and turned those one-day tickets into annual passes for everyone; so our first year in Pasadena we spent many Fridays exploring Disneyland. It only took about six weeks for the kids to decide that this new place was okay. Even though we were stuck in an awkward rental house for a year with much less space than before, they had started to feel at home.

About the second or third month after the family had joined me, we were driving home from a family Friday at the beach and our youngest child, Sophie, was talking in the van about how much she missed her best friend back in Richardson. She announced to all of us, "Someday I'm going to move back to Texas and live with my friend Taryn." In unison, her three older brothers turned around and said, "No way! We're never moving back. This place is awesome!" It took a handful of Fridays, but I knew in that moment the transition, at least for three out of the six of us, was almost complete.

Obviously, Friday adventures are a little easier to come up with in an area like Los Angeles than they might be in some other places, but there are all kinds of little ways you can help your family begin to feel connected to a new location. Some of our very best Friday adventures here have been things that exist everywhere: farmers' markets, street fairs, and high school football games.

If you are a pastor, more often than not the church will work at helping you feel at home, and because you are immediately immersed in ministry, you will quickly have more relationships than you can manage. Take the time, however, to make sure your family feels as connected to a new location as you do.

ESTABLISH CLEAR EXPECTATIONS

Pastor Adams was excited to get a fresh start in her new ministry assignment. In her first pastorate she had developed habits of procrastination and pulling things together at the last minute that she was anxious to break. She was determined in her new church to get off to a diligent, organized, and focused start. Because she wanted to make sure things in her first services operated smoothly, she took care of every detail of the worship preparation. She even went so far as to fold the bulletins and prepare the eucharistic elements. Because there was so much to do, she decided not to take a day off for the first few weeks and to schedule as many appointments as she could. She deeply wanted to get to know the congregation, so she had her assistant schedule at least four or five meals with people each week. For the first six months she attended every high school sporting event, accepted every invitation to serve on a community board, personally called on every sick parishioner, and even spent her Saturdays working with the yard and custodial volunteers making sure the church was spick-and-span for Sunday. The first six months could not have gone any better. People were amazed at all of her energy. They had no idea that they had called Wonder Woman to be their pastor.

But at the end of six months Pastor Adams was exhausted. She faced a daunting and embarrassing problem. Because she had been doing so much work in worship preparation, pastoral care, community activism, and even facility maintenance, she had set a bar of ministry for herself that she did not have the stamina to continue to jump over. And even worse, because she was doing almost everything, there were very few volunteers who were coming alongside her to carry the load. She had set new habits, but she was also close to burning out after only half a year.

Changing ministry locations is often a wonderful blessing. Transitions always give a leader a chance for a new start. They are an opportunity to set new habits and achieve new levels of discipline. But it is extremely important to remember that although your new church has some built-in expectations of any pastor, most of their expectations of you will be set by you in the first hundred days or so. It is important that you work hard in the earliest days to make an appropriate positive first impression. (First impressions are extremely hard to overcome.) But it is also vital that you establish early on patterns and expectations that you will be able to live with over the long haul of ministry. Michael G. McBride has said that most congregations believe that the model pastor

- Preaches exactly twenty minutes then sits down.

- Condemns sin but never hurts anyone's feelings.

- Works from eight in the morning until ten in the evening but never gets tired.
- Is 26 years old and has been preaching for 30 years.
- Has a burning desire to work with the teenagers but spends much time with senior citizens.
- Makes fifteen calls a day on church members, yet evangelizes the unchurched at a record pace.
- Does all of the above without ever being out of the office when you call![15]

You can help a congregation have healthier expectations of you if you will be as clear as you can in the beginning about what they should expect. Here are a few things I would suggest you do in the first hundred days to help form appropriate expectations.

First, I would suggest working with the church's leadership board to form a very clear job or ministry description. I prefer to call these *ministry covenants* because, as I have mentioned earlier, pastors are called to be part of the community, so I prefer to think of these arrangements as a mutual covenant of faithfulness between a pastor and his or her congregation rather than as a job description. But no matter what they are titled, it is critical for there to be a clear set of expectations articulated between a pastor and those to whom he or she is most clearly accountable.

I think a good way of going through this process is to ask the board to give you a first draft of their covenantal expectations of you as pastor based on their past expectations and their understanding of their current needs. You could then ask permission to take that first draft and reflect on it and pray about it and then rework it in ways that best fit your giftedness and your ability to faithfully fulfill their expectations. You could next give that revised covenant back to the group of leaders and give them time to agree with your revisions or to suggest alterations. It may take all of the first one hundred days to come to agreement on the final form of the ministry description or covenant. But I believe that work will pay off. There are few things worse than having a church board disappointed in you as their pastor because you did not fulfill expectations that were unspoken and unwritten. It also makes moments of assessment far easier and more just when there is a clear list of covenant expectations that can be evaluated.

It is very important to create a workable time schedule and stick to it as closely as you can for the first hundred days. It might even be wise after setting your office hours to publish them for a few weeks in the worship folder or church bulletin.

It is important that in your schedule you establish a clear day off during the week. Because for most pastors Saturdays and Sundays are workdays, most ministers will choose to take a weekday as a day of rest. Mondays or Fridays seem to be the most popular days for pastors to take a break. I prefer to take Friday rather than Monday off—and I encourage my pastoral staff to do the same. I choose this approach because after all that happens on Sunday, I am emotionally exhausted on most Mondays and would prefer to work when I'm tired and spend time with my family when I can be fully present with them. So I ask my staff to give me their tired day and give their family their best day. Also, it has been my experience that Sunday tends to shake things loose for some people in the congregation. The Holy Spirit will often speak to somebody during worship on Sunday, but then the person will need to process that with someone Monday morning. I also like to meet with staff on Monday while the services from the weekend are fresh in our minds and while there is a week ahead to plan. (I also like to be in the office on Monday so I know what the offering and attendance totals were from the day before.)

Which day you choose to take off is not as important as the fact that you pick a day and try to stick to it. The church knows that Friday is my day off and that I try hard to keep it sacred as a time of rest and as a time for family. Obviously, there are exceptions. Ministry is a calling and not a job, so in some sense every twenty-four-hour period is open to the various contingencies that the life of a pastor may encounter. But try hard to keep that day sacred.

My wife and I use the "scale from one to ten" game as a way to communicate what events are most important to us. If something is a one or two, it is not important at all. But if something is a nine or a ten, then we understand that only death can keep us from being present for the other. My assistant knows it takes something that is an eight or above to get me to violate sacred Fridays.

Your congregation needs to know that sermon or teaching preparation is a high value for you, so you need to reserve clear times to use for study. I try to be working several weeks ahead in sermon preparation, but I still try to set aside at least a couple hours on Monday and Tuesday afternoons for this purpose. I like to have my studying done so I can be preparing mentally and spiritually for Sunday throughout the week. But also because of the need for my print, worship, and technical teams to have time to prepare, the sooner I am ready, the more time they have to be creative and get their work done. Helping the congregation know from the beginning that you need time for sermon preparation is important, and my assistant knows it takes a six or above to get me to violate sacred study time.

In addition to setting a clear schedule, you will probably want to limit the number of outside invitations you accept in the early days of transition. Community organizations and church groups will be anxious to involve a new pastor in many boards and committees. It is important to get involved, and the invitations always feel like a great honor. But during your first hundred days your focus should be on getting off to a good start at the church, and so make additional commitments slowly.

I also think it is wise at various times during the first hundred days to reflect from the pulpit on a biblical vision for the church and for ministry. I began my tenure at Pasadena First Church by preaching a series on 1 John titled "What Does a Good Church Look Like?" I wish I could tell you I had planned that carefully. The truth is, I had already been working on the series and was planning to preach it at my former church, so I just preached what I intended for my old assignment in my new one. But in retrospect, it was unintentionally wise to spend the first several weeks exploring the biblical vision for how the body of Christ ought to function in its life together, and by extension what the pastor's role within the church ought to be. The more you can help the church understand your theological vision for ministry in your early days with them, the better off you will be.

I once saw a church sign that read, "Welcome to City Church. Senior Pastor: Reverend Thompson. Ministers: Everyone Else." I really like that sign and the theology from Ephesians that undergirds it:

> So Christ himself gave the apostles, the prophets, the evangelists, the pastors and teachers, to equip his people for works of service, so that the body of Christ may be built up until we all reach unity in the faith and in the knowledge of the Son of God and become mature, attaining to the whole measure of the fullness of Christ. (Eph. 4:11-13)

In the first hundred days help the church have the right expectations of how you will work to "equip his people for works of service" and it will help you establish good patterns that can be sustained in the years to come.

If you have a spouse, I think it is important to have a conversation with the leadership board about the expectations the church can and will have of him or her. Again, because ministry is a calling and not merely a job, the spouse of a pastor cannot help but be involved at some level in the ministry of their wife or husband.

But the expectations on the spouse of a minister can sometimes be unfair.

In the interview process with the leadership board and during the first hundred days with the congregation I would articulate clearly what strengths God has given your spouse and what ways he or she likes to participate in your ministry. But if you have young children, if your spouse works outside the home, or if your spouse prefers to be involved in places in the community, the expectations of the church need to be tempered by the other constraints on his or her time.

It is not only critical that the congregation have the right expectations of you and your family but also important that you have a clear understanding of how the church will respond back to you in covenantal faithfulness. It always seems a little bit awkward, but it is essential that early on in the process you have clear and direct conversations about salary and various other areas of compensation.

Pastors very rarely get wealthy, but they frequently go broke, so it is vital for your good and for the financial health of your family that you know how your financial needs will be cared for. Do not be afraid in the interview process to ask for the compensation package in writing so that you can work on a budget and figure out if you will be able to afford to make a transition.

Housing is always a tricky aspect of a pastor's salary. Some churches still have parsonages that are available for a pastoral family to live in. If that is the case, be clear about what expenses are yours and which are covered by the church. Does the church cover any of the utility costs? What repairs and what level of maintenance are you expected to cover? Although a parsonage can save a church a great deal of money, it also prevents a pastor from building equity, which can greatly limit his or her future opportunities and damage his or her retirement. Is the church willing to add additional resources to the pastor's retirement fund or into a savings account to help the pastor build some equity?

If the church does not have a parsonage, is there a housing allowance as part of the salary? Often churches put housing and salary together and the pastor is responsible for determining what portion of the salary is designated as housing for the purposes of tax relief. If this is the case, you need to make sure the salary and housing are sufficient to be able to live without going into increasing debt. Especially if you are moving into a community where housing and other expenses are significantly higher, it is important to use cost-of-living calculations to make sure that what appears to be an increase in salary on paper is actually sufficient to meet additional living expenses.

Other important financial expectations to be clear on are

- Does the church pay for the pastor's social security?
- Is there a pension program, and does the church contribute to it for the pastor?
- Are there any allowances for car expenses, mileage, or cell phone costs?
- Is there a budget given to the pastor for pastoral expenses such as books, travel, conferences, and church-related meals?
- What are the expectations with regard to participation in denominational meetings or assemblies, and is money set aside to cover those expenses?

- How much vacation time do you receive? Are the number of vacation weeks set or do they increase over time? What is the sick leave policy? Are there weeks in which taking vacation is not permitted? And does the church have a sabbatical policy?

- Is medical insurance covered by the church or is it the responsibility of the pastor? Is the pastor's family covered or does the pastor need to pay to have the family covered? Are other benefits included such as dental, eye care, disability, or life insurance?

I am sure that there are other questions that should be added to this list. The point is that in the first hundred days make sure church members are learning what they should expect from you and be clear on what you can expect from them as you walk in covenant together.

PREACH
WELL

Next to helping your family transition well, I believe the highest priority for the pastor in the first hundred days of transition is to preach, teach, and prepare worship well. In the Old Testament there were three significant offices of spiritual leadership among the people of God: the prophet, the priest, and the king. In many ways the pastor has to serve all three of these important leadership functions.

The pastor, like a good king, needs to be a good manager of people, resources, and the future direction of the church. The priestly functions of blessing, counseling, and care are extremely significant for the pastor. But I am convinced that the unique and central role of the minister is the prophetic one. The care the pastor gives to speaking for and about God to the people under his or her care will largely shape the people's impressions of how a pastor fulfills all of his or her other roles as well. Lawrence Farris says it well:

> Not only is preaching the way the new pastor touches the most people at one time with the message of God's grace and justice and compassion, it is the unique and distinctive function of the pastor. . . . Most congregants will form their first impressions of a new pastor based upon her work as a preacher, so it is helpful to other aspects of a pastor's ministry to preach and lead worship well. Many church members will assume that if she does a good job leading worship, she will probably also do other ministerial tasks well. Conversely, if worship is led poorly, folks will start to wonder what, if anything, the minister does well.[16]

Every preacher has a somewhat unique way to approach the task of proclaiming the Word of God to the church, but let me suggest five things I think are really important for preaching during the first hundred days.

First, start your preaching ministry at a new church with material you are comfortable with. Between family demands, unpacking boxes, setting up the office, and meeting with new people, the actual time a pastor in a new assignment has for sermon preparation is usually very limited. The first three months are probably not the best time to develop the in-depth series you have been dying to do on the book of Leviticus. Time will be short and valuable, and so it might be wise to begin with material you have either used before in another location, or, if it is your first ministry assignment, to preach from texts that are familiar enough to you that you aren't starting your exegesis from scratch.

Being comfortable with the material also will help you to preach well when you will likely be a bit nervous. My wife likes to tease me about what she calls my "sugar-stick" sermons and illustrations. She knows there are sermons and stories I have used enough that they are uniquely mine, I know they are filled with important truth, and I know how to communicate them effectively. So she knows when big moments come along, like the first few Sundays at a new church, that I will more than likely pull out my "sugar-stick" sermons. There is nothing wrong with that. You want to get off to a good preaching start.

Second, I think it is important in the first hundred days to preach vision. It is too early in your tenure in your new ministry to have a specific agenda for the direction of the church, but you can begin to articulate a theological vision for the church. When I was a college professor, we used to have a retreat at the end of the year for graduating seniors in the theology and ministry department. We would use the retreat as a time of commissioning and blessing for the students, but we would also use it as a time of assessment for those of us who were teaching in the School of Theology and Ministry. Before the retreat we would give each student a written assignment meant to assess what he or she had learned from us. This essay exam had only one question on it. Each student was to write his or her response to this question: "What does a good church look like?" I think that is a great question.

Richard J. Mouw, the president of Fuller Theological Seminary, has shared with me the three most important questions that inform his task as a seminary president. The three questions are, (1) What is God doing in the world? (2) What does the church look like that understands what God is doing in the world? And (3) what does the seminary look like that is forming people to lead the church that understands what God is doing in the world? I love those three questions.

Take some time and reflect on these questions. What does a good church look like? What is God doing in the world? And what does the church look like that understands what God is doing in the world? I am convinced these are the kinds of questions that are central to the task of a pastor, and I think these are the kinds of questions that ought to inform the sermons you preach during the first hundred days in a new location of ministry.

As I shared in a previous chapter, the first series I preached in my current assignment was on 1 John and was titled "What Does a Good Church Look Like?" I was so glad—even if I wasn't wise enough to plan it—that my tenure began with setting a theological vision from the Scripture for what a good church looks like. I hope I don't make another ministry transition, but if I do, my guess is that I will pull that series out again, rework it, and make it the first set of sermons in that new location. First John isn't the only place to start. Here are some places where other pastors begin:

- Pastor Rob begins with sermons from Exodus on what it means for God to hear the cries of the oppressed, to redeem them by his grace, to make them a new creation by his sacrificial love, to form them into a new people as they pass through the waters, and to shape their character in the wilderness and by his law.

- Pastor Beth preaches a series on the Psalms of Ascent (Pss. 120–34), based on Eugene Peterson's book *A Long Journey in the Same Direction,* in order to emphasize that the transformation God wants to bring to the church happens in worship, happens as the community walks before the Lord together, and happens—not in an instant—but over the long haul as the church journeys in faith toward the goal of sanctification and holiness he has for his people.

- Pastor Jon entered into a very broken church, and so he spent the first eight weeks preaching from the prophetic texts of hope beginning with Isa. 40 and Ezek. 37.

- Pastor David begins his new ministry by preaching from Isa. 11 about what it means to be a "lion and lamb" community.

- Pastor Robin begins her tenure at a new church by preaching a series from the Sermon on the Mount in Matthew because she sees this as the perfect place from which to proclaim Christ's vision for his kingdom.

- Pastor Davis uses the seven churches in Rev. 2 and 3 as a way to describe the kind of spirit Christ desires his church to have.

There are all kinds of places to go in Scripture to find the vision for God's people. The point is simply that without a vision people perish, and so one of the first things a new pastor can accomplish in his or her preaching is to cast a theological vision for the church as it moves forward into the new days God has for it.

Preaching in ways that reveal something about yourself and your family is the third suggestion for preaching during the first hundred days. The majority of people in a congregation care deeply for their pastor and his or her family. People want to know about you and what your family dynamics are like. They want to be able to identify with you.

When our oldest son was born, my dad sent me a cartoon in the mail of a minister looking over the crib at his newborn baby and saying, "How is my little sermon illustration doing today?" Some of us who grew up in the parsonage may not think that cartoon is very funny, but we know there is a great deal of truth to it. I try to be extremely careful to only tell stories about my family that cast them in a good light, but I realize people want to know what the members of my family are like. And I want the people in the congregation to know that we are a normal family and that we are mutual travelers through life with them.

The life of the preacher cannot serve as his or her only source of illustrations, but I would encourage you, especially in the early days of a new ministry, to preach in ways that are self-disclosing and let people know about you.

My fourth suggestion is that as you reveal things about yourself, you also preach in ways that are self-effacing. The congregation wants to know about you, but there is nothing more obnoxious than a preacher who is always the hero in his or her own stories. A preacher who can laugh at his or her own mistakes becomes real and approachable for those who sit under his or her ministry. I am convinced a church can only move forward on its knees as it is able to live in a posture of confession. But I am also convinced a church will ultimately reflect the vulnerability and transparency of its leader. That doesn't mean a preacher ought to drag out his or her dirty laundry every Sunday, but it does mean the pastor's humility before God should be reflected in the spirit with which the pastor talks about his or her life.

As a general rule, when I talk about others—especially my family—I try to make sure I only cast them in a good light, but when I talk about myself I try to be appropriately humble and self-effacing.

Finally, in the first hundred days the pastor in a new setting needs to focus not just on preaching but also on every aspect of the service: scripture, prayer, sacraments, and even benedictions. I will come back to the issue of change in a later chapter, but I would not change a whole lot about the tone and format of worship that a church is used to in the first hundred days. The word "culture" comes from Latin word *cultus* meaning "worship." It is from this same word that we get the word "cult." A culture is formed in the ways we worship and through the practices people use that show honor to individuals or institutions. It should not surprise us then that in the church people get used to a culture of worship, and adjustments to those practices often make people nervous and out of sorts. Even little changes in worship can have major reactions.

Pastor Todd was convinced that the proper liturgical location for receiving tithes and offerings was at the end of the worship service. And so on his second Sunday at his new church the only alteration he made to the order of worship was to move the offering from just before the morning message to the end of the worship service. The first week he made the change, no one said anything positive or negative. The second week the offering came at the end of the service, he received two anonymous letters in the mail complaining about the changes he was making to the worship service. After the third week of concluding worship with the offering Pastor Todd found himself Sunday afternoon in a spontaneously called crisis meeting of the church board, the volunteer music director, the church treasurer, and the team of ushers. The music director was upset because the new location for the offering was putting too much pressure on her to pick powerful offertories. The church treasurer was angry because he could no longer count the offering during the sermon but now had to stay after church or come back later in the week to count the tithes. Some of the ushers liked the change, but others missed having all of their work accomplished before the sermon started. And a few members of the board were upset because they were convinced that putting the offering at the end of the service meant the new pastor would never end the service with an altar call.

Even in nonliturgical church settings, people get used to a culture of worship, so my suggestion would be that in the first hundred days you make few changes to the culture, order, and style of worship the church is used to. You will eventually make alterations to the practice of worship in the church you lead, but the changes you make should be done slowly and by clearly articulating the thoughtful (and theological) reasons behind making those changes.

But even as you work within the current liturgical order and culture, it is important to plan the worship well and to think about how the various aspects of the service will be performed.

The reading of Scripture is central to worship. It is important to find out how this church is used to approaching the reading of the Bible. How much Scripture is usually read in the service and who reads it? Do people stand as the Scripture is read or are they used to sitting? Does the congregation have a habit of reading responsively? What translation is the congregation used to reading from? Are there Bibles in the pew racks for people to use? Are the texts read during worship included on screens or printed in the bulletin?

People will rarely complain that Scripture is being given a more prominent place in worship. So think through how the role of the reading of the Word will be included in the early days of your worship direction.

Prayer is a significant part of the church's culture of worship. How is the church used to praying? Is there a time of pastoral prayer during the service? Are prayers written or spontaneous? Does the church make use of altars or kneelers during prayer? What is the church's view and practice of anointing with oil? Are prayer requests made known to the congregation prior to prayer, and if so, how are they collected and distributed? Is the church used to praying the Lord's Prayer as part of the worship?

In the first weeks of a ministry the pastor needs to carefully think through practices of prayer that fit within the culture of the congregation but also allow the pastor to express his or her priestly concern for the people and invite the Spirit of God to enter into the life and needs of the congregation in meaningful ways.

Part of the role of the pastor is to take authority to administer the sacraments. Discover what the church is used to regarding the sacraments. How often does the church practice baptism? Where do baptisms take place? What methods (sprinkling, pouring, or immersion) is the congregation used to? Is the congregation used to baptizing infants or are they used to baptizing only adults? What has been the preferred method for preparing people for baptism? How often has the Lord's Supper been served to the congregation in the past? What method for receiving the Eucharist is the congregation used to? Who usually prepares the elements?

It is important to prepare well for administering the sacraments. These are high and holy moments when the minister gets to handle some of the most significant "means of grace" for God's people. It is important to consider how a congregation is used to approaching these moments, but it is also important that early on a new pastor form patterns that demonstrate the significance he or she gives to the sacraments.

I would encourage you to also think through how you want to bless the people. Some churches are used to benedictions; others are not. Even if they are not, I have never found the inclusion of a benediction at the end of the service to be a reason for tension. Even if they have never experienced it, most people quickly grow to desire receiving a prayer of blessing as they leave a time of worship. There are many biblical benedictions to choose from. And it is not inappropriate to write a benediction of one's own. But I think it is important for a pastor to conclude worship by blessing the people.

At every level, first impressions are important. But nowhere are first impressions more important for a new minister than in preaching and worship. I want to emphasize again that each church has a culture of worship it is used to, and I think it is wise to move slowly as you make changes to that culture. It is critical in a new setting for a pastor to prepare to preach well and to think carefully through all the aspects of worship so that a new congregation will leave the first hundred days trusting that the spiritual future of their church has been placed in the right hands.

SECURE SOME EARLY WINS

In the next chapter—chapter 7—I will deal with the critical issue of making changes, but no matter what changes a pastor ultimately wants to make, the ability to enact change in a new ministry setting is in direct proportion to the amount of credibility a pastor can build up for himself or herself in the early days of ministry. The credibility necessary to enact change in an organization is often referred to as social capital. Like monetary capital needed to make significant investments, social capital is the goodwill of the people that is earned and accumulated by a leader and can be used when difficult transitions need to be made.

Leadership specialist Michael Watkins argues that one of the fastest ways for a new leader to accelerate the accumulation of social capital is to secure what he calls early wins. "Early wins excite and energize people and build your personal credibility."[17] Early wins are those moments when the best parts of your true heart are revealed to the people and allow you to immediately begin to earn large amounts of social capital.

Perhaps the easiest and best place to garner some early wins is in the area of pastoral care. As soon as you arrive, get a list of the people who are in the hospital and go and visit them. In the first few Sundays of your tenure most people connected with the church will come to a service because they will want to see and meet the new pastor and his or her family. But those families that have a loved one in the hospital will often not be able to attend, and they will feel disconnected from you. It is vital that you get to know them and express your concern for them and take the opportunity to pray with them.

It would also be a good idea to get a list of those who are part of the church but because of illness or age are homebound or living in a rehabilitation or care center and visit them. If you feel comfortable, it is a good practice after your first Sunday when the Lord's Supper is served to take elements with you to visit those who are shut-ins and express to them that they have not been forgotten and are no less a part of the body of Christ. It is also a good idea during this first round of visits to those who are homebound to take a picture or pictures of your family with you so that they know what your spouse and children look like. This is an important gesture of connection, but I have also found that some of the best prayer warriors in a church are those who are unable to be out and about. I want them praying for my family and for me. You will be amazed at how caring for these often forgotten people will quickly garner good gossip for you in the community and affirm your desire to be the pastor of the whole church. Often people who are aged and ill are fearful that a transition in ministry will mean they will be forgotten. Alleviating those very real concerns will be an easy early win.

People who have recently experienced loss are also often fearful that a transition in pastoral leadership will mean their pain will be forgotten. More than likely one of your predecessors in ministry walked with them through a time of great loss and made a significant connection with them during that time of grief. They will naturally be concerned that you will not understand or share their loneliness.

My wife came up with two ideas that have helped me accumulate a great deal of social capital. Our first Sunday in Pasadena happened to be Palm Sunday. Immediately my wife asked for a list of all the people in the church who had lost a spouse or child in the last year or two. She had tulips sent to them on Good Friday with a card that simply said, "We understand that you have gone through a significant time of loss. Remember, it's Friday, but Sunday's coming. You are loved. Scott and Debbie Daniels." I believe there were twelve people who were on the list the first year. By the Tuesday after Easter I had received twelve calls or notes thanking me for my love and concern and for knowing about their loss. I also had twelve new friends who were glad to have me as their pastor. The tulips are now a yearly tradition.

Debbie also had the idea in our first year that the two of us should host a Valentine's lunch for all the widows and widowers of the church. We encouraged them to invite others they knew who were also in their situation. It was a lovely occasion and a beautiful way to express care. It was instantaneously a major source of good gossip and social capital. It, too, has become an annual tradition.

People trust those who they believe love them and have their best interest in mind. The quickest ways to build trust and to garner early wins is through pastoral care.

Another way to establish early wins is to be relational. It may be a significant challenge during the first hundred days, but in those first weeks find ways to be connected in as many relationships with the congregation as possible.

It may take you more than three months to get ready, but as soon as you can get things together, begin to invite people into your home. By nature people are curious and inquisitive, and the majority of the people in a congregation want to know how and where your family lives. When we are as close as we can be to being established and having pictures on the wall, Debbie and I host an open house for the congregation. As our areas of ministry and now our churches have grown larger, it has become a much bigger ordeal. (In our last open house we sent flowers to all our neighbors ahead of time to apologize for the invasion they were about to experience.) But we have believed the effort is always worth it. Beyond curiosity, people in a church want to know that they are caring for their pastoral families and that the families are feeling at home in the community. An open house is a good way, early on, to take care of the whole church at once.

If you can't do it all at once, schedule a regular time (perhaps once a month or so) when you will invite a small group of people over. I have a friend who takes the list of members and systematically goes through the alphabet and invites six to eight individuals to their house per month in order to get connected. Another one of my wife's great ideas is to start a birthday club. She takes one Saturday morning per month and hosts a brunch at our home for all the ladies in the church who have birthdays during that month. It is not only a great way to connect relationally with others but also an interesting way to mix up various generations in the church. Every month ladies get to know someone they have never met before.

I have a pastor friend who plays golf every Monday morning at 8:00 a.m. and gets the course to book two or three consecutive tee times; anyone who wants to come and play golf with the pastor knows there is an open spot every Monday morning. Another friend during his first year at a new church ate lunch every Tuesday in the same café and reserved a table large enough for anyone who wanted to come and have lunch with the new pastor.

I pray my benediction on Sunday morning while walking down the aisle so that I can be at the back door to shake hands as everyone leaves. There are three back doors to the church's sanctuary, so I switch doors every week so that I can get to know everyone's face. Some Sundays I skip the doors and go to the base of the balcony stairs so that I can shake hands with the people who sit in the balcony. I love how shocked their faces are as they descend from the stairs and run into me. Even though, by the time the last service is over, I have had a really long morning, being relational and available is a source of early and easy wins.

A new and developing area for being relational is the cyberworld. A few years ago I started a blog and I am fascinated by the number of people inside and outside the congregation that read it. Seminars are now being taught regularly on how pastors can effectively use social networking sites—like Facebook—to stay connected to parishioners. You want to be judicious in your use of electronic media. Sometimes we write things in emails or blogs that we wouldn't say face-to-face, and once they are out on the net they are gone forever, but nevertheless, this may be an important tool in the future for pastors to use to stay connected.

One way of garnering an easy win with your leadership team or board is to run a good meeting. Running a long, disorganized, ineffective meeting is one of the quickest ways to lose credibility with strong leaders. But leading a timely, thoughtful, and productive meeting will be an important early win with some of the most significant individuals with whom you need to build social capital.

Business guru Patrick Lencioni writes some of my favorite books on how to conduct meetings. In his book *Death by Meeting: A Leadership Fable About Solving the Most Painful Problem in Business* Lencioni argues that meetings should function like a good television sitcom or drama.[18] Each week people tune into their favorite television comedy or drama and they know the characters, they know roughly how the timing of the program will go, and they know that the plot will resolve, and yet each week they tune in with excitement to see what will happen. In the same way, argues Lencioni, meetings should be something leaders look forward to. They happen the same time each week or month. They should have a clear plot or agenda. They should have a fixed time frame to get the work accomplished. And enough preparation should go into the meeting that the things being decided on are dramatic and worthy of a leader's involvement.

It may take some time to form good meetings that people look forward to. If a church leadership team or board has spent years in long meetings dealing with trivial things, chances are the most capable and talented leaders in the church no longer are willing to serve on the board. But the better organized, more focused, and more significant—as a leader—you can help your meetings become, the more credibility and social capital you will gain with your most important long-term agents of change in the church.

My last suggestion here would be that you find one area where you can pick up some early wins and focus some effort there. In many situations this easy area of credibility will be with the church facility itself. Frequently during a time of ministry transition a church building will be neglected. The yard work is ignored. Walls go unpainted. Stacks of miscellaneous materials get shoved into corners. Don't do all the work yourself, and don't chop down the tree John Wesley planted, but find easy ways to enhance the facility and put together a workday so that the community can come together and weed, mow, paint, sort, and throw out so that the church looks as new as possible. Most congregants deeply appreciate when a new pastor treats the church facility with the same care he or she treats his or her own home.

Many of my pastor friends have suggested that one area of early focus that helps gain credibility is to pay attention to the children and youth ministries. Again, during times of interim, these are two areas of ministry that sometimes get neglected. One of the things that drove my wife crazy at a new church was the outdated nature of the toys, swings, and cribs in the nursery area. And so after making sure there weren't any sacred cows dwelling in the nursery area, we threw a shower for the nursery and filled it with new materials so that families with babies and toddlers would know that this church cared for their children.

Some pastors decide during their first few months to include children's sermons in the worship time so that the kids feel special during worship. I have a friend who asked permission of the volunteer youth leader to lead the youth Sunday school class for the first three months. The volunteer gladly obliged. These months gave the pastor time to get to know the young people in the church but more importantly to make a statement to their families that she was a pastor who not only ministered to the "big people" but also cared deeply for the young people who were both the present and the future of the church.

Expressing concern for people's children is a key place for early wins.

There may be other areas that fit with the pastor's gifting that will add credibility. My minor in my doctoral work was in church history. It is a favorite subject of mine. I decided during the first few months at the church to teach a Wednesday night class on church history. I knew it was a subject that people did not know much about and that I could teach easily and well. It was a delightful series of classes that not only helped me connect with people but also helped them discover my depth and interests in ways they may not have done without the class.

Find the ways that work best for you. But the more you can fill your social bank account with wins during the first hundred days, the sooner you will have the necessary credibility and trust to move the church through the challenges and changes in the days to come.

CHOOSE YOUR BATTLES CAREFULLY

I can only remember a handful of chapels from my years as a student at Northwest Nazarene College, but one of the speakers I remember vividly spoke on Christ's call to his disciples to "take up their cross daily and follow" him (Luke 9:23). The point of his message was that Jesus invites his followers not only to live well but also to die well. The challenge, this speaker pointed out, was deciding what cross was worthy of dying on. It is easy to pick an unworthy cross.

I'm not completely sold now on the speaker's exegesis of Luke 9:23. But the point of the message continues to ring true with me nevertheless. In ministry there are things worth battling for and even dying for. But there are many pastors who have given up their ministries by fighting unnecessary battles. I don't just mean having the privileges of ministry taken away due to acts of immorality—although those are clearly choices not worth losing everything for. What I mean to focus on are the unfortunate ideas, agendas, and strategies that become unnecessary sources of conflict and often the cross upon which a ministry dies.

Falls Creek Church of the Nazarene was a church of three hundred but knew it could easily be a church of six or seven hundred. While they were interviewing for a new pastor, they became impressed with Pastor Ron, a young pastor who in his interview had articulated a ninety-day strategy for change. He had read a couple best-selling business books on turning over troubled businesses in a hurry and decided that many of the strategies articulated there could work as well to bring about transformation in the church. Interestingly, when he shared some of his ideas for change in the interview process, the board was very impressed. He admitted that his proposed agenda was aggressive and that the church might initially lose a few people. Nevertheless, he believed that those who didn't want to change would be the few who would leave. And, he argued, getting rid of those who were fixed in old patterns would ultimately be a good thing. The church could consider it the pruning that is necessary for new growth to begin. So he told the board that if he came as pastor, the church might have to "choose who to lose" but that the dramatic changes would bring in the new people necessary for the church to get to the next level. Many of the business people on the board resonated with his knowledge of organizational change and were very excited about his obvious drive to "make things happen." And so he was called unanimously to be the new pastor.

Before his first Sunday in his new position he had mapped out the three main agenda items for his ninety-day strategy for change. The first item on the to-do list was to reduce the size of the formal leadership team. There were currently sixteen members on the board of directors for the church. Everything Pastor Ron read in the business world said that smaller leadership teams are more effective because they can make decisions expeditiously and they are able to mobilize into action quickly. And so, Pastor Ron spent the little bit of initial social capital given to him as a new pastor to push through a congregational vote in his second week that reduced the size of the board from sixteen to ten for the upcoming church elections. Unfortunately, in the new election four of Pastor Ron's most vocal initial supporters were not reelected to the leadership board. Two of those four who were not reelected were significant financial contributors, and they were now quite hurt by the outcome and blamed the new pastor for their alienation from leadership.

The second part of the change agenda was to quickly make necessary alterations to the pastoral staff. Pastor Ron spent the first month carefully assessing the strengths and qualities of the current church staff. There were six other pastors that made up the pastoral team. At the end of thirty days, he decided that three of the six were not a good fit for the new direction the church was going to take. And so, with the permission of the board of directors, he released three of the six from ministry, graciously (he thought) giving each one a check for three months of severance. Then he quickly began the process of looking for replacements.

Unfortunately one of the pastors he terminated had been on staff at the church for twenty-three years and was deeply connected to most of the senior adults in the church, and so, to the older generation, this pastor's release felt not just like an act of disloyalty but like a direct affront to all of the older adults in the church. They were suspicious from the start that this new youthful pastor only cared about the young people, and for them this particular staff decision only confirmed their suspicions.

Unbeknownst to Pastor Ron, one of the other pastors he let go was related by marriage to three of the pillar families of the church. Their concern for their relative's damaged future in ministry made them irate with this new pastor who had just arrived on the scene and, at least in their minds, had let their loved one go without cause.

The third pastor who was fired was actually thrilled to be let go. For a number of years he had been leading a young adult Sunday school class. Many of the members of the class were very discontent with the way the church had been going for some time. They were, however, very loyal to this pastor who had taught them, performed several of their marriage ceremonies, and dedicated many of their babies. For a number of years it had been his dream to start his own church, and he now saw this as his opportunity. He took his severance money, moved down the road three miles, and started his own church with forty of the members of his former Sunday school class and their families.

Pastor Ron's final agenda for change was to make the church and its services more seeker friendly. He believed the church needed to do two things to accomplish this. It needed to change its name, and it needed to make the worship service more contemporary. So he paid a graphic artist to work with some of his ideas, and on his sixth Sunday morning at the church he presented the artist's drawings for his new proposal. He informed the congregation that the name Falls Creek Church of the Nazarene was not a good name for the future of the church. For one thing, the church was no longer in Falls Creek, but now, in its third different location, it actually fell within the boundaries of the city of Cedar Lane. Second, the latest studies by church growth experts reveal that most nonbelievers are very apprehensive about entering a church with a denominational name in its title. Most people, he argued, view denominational titles as an obstacle to coming to Christ. Therefore, he unveiled a large poster complete with the graphic concepts for the new name he would like to propose for the church. Falls Creek Church of the Nazarene would now be called Cedar Lane New Life Community. He even pointed out that the initials CLNLC were reversible and so work well not only in graphics but also as a domain name.

The reactions from the congregation could not have been worse. One family whose grandfather had planted the original church in Falls Creek saw the name change as a slap in the face to the heritage of their ancestors. At least a third of the people there that morning, those that were deeply committed to the denomination, immediately saw this as a sign that their new pastor was not loyal in the least to the church's tradition or its theological foundations.

Five people who were new to the church kind of liked the idea, but it seemed that everyone else was upset about it, in part because they weren't even shown the courtesy of being consulted about this important decision.

Pastor Ron's plans next involved moving the service from traditional to contemporary worship. The church was clearly stuck in a worship style that did not meet the tastes of the majority of the community around them. Pastor Ron knew it was the right thing to do, but he worried about how to enact some of the changes. For example, who was going to tell the long-time organist that she was no longer needed? This ended up not being a problem because the organist left the church over the name change. On Pastor Ron's first Sunday at the church there had been 327 people in worship. On the first Sunday of the new contemporary worship format—Pastor Ron's tenth Sunday as pastor —there were 143 people in worship. That is, until the music started. When the electric guitar struck the first chord and the drums boomed in on the down beat, 22 more people walked out.

Soon Pastor Ron and the remaining church staff were having difficult staff meetings each Monday. The meetings became long discussions about how horrible the people of the church were and how they loved their traditions more than they loved God. Because the overwhelming majority of the feedback he was receiving was negative, Pastor Ron began to take on a bit of a martyr complex and he began to withdraw emotionally and relationally from those who remained at the church.

Within a month the board of ten lay leaders contacted the local denominational supervisor and called an emergency meeting with Pastor Ron. The board decided that their only choice was to terminate their relationship with their new pastor and give him six months worth of severance. Pastor Ron had come in with a dynamic ninety-day agenda for change—an agenda embraced by the church leadership—but within those three months he was gone. The church had certainly changed. It had a new name, half the people, half of its original staff, angry laity, and all of its cash reserves paid out in severance expenses.

The story of Pastor Ron and the Falls Creek Church is 100 percent fictional, but I can name about a dozen churches where almost this identical situation has taken place, and you probably can too.

On the one hand, it could be argued that every change Pastor Ron was trying to implement was the correct one. For a time the leadership team even agreed with him. The obvious problem was the speed at which Pastor Ron was trying to implement systematic changes, and the second problem was his inability to choose correctly and wisely which battles to fight and when.

There are several common mistakes pastors at a new church make that inhibit their ability to bring transformation and may even lead quickly to the destruction of their credibility for ministry. Here are some of the most common errors new pastors make:

- Being a know-it-all. Pastors have a tendency to graduate from seminary or come home from a powerful seminar and feel convinced they now know how to make things work well. This often gives church people the impression that they are ignorant or backward, and no one responds well to a sense of being belittled.

- Making immediate, sweeping changes sends the message to congregation members that every-thing they have been doing is wrong. Cultures can change, but they change slowly.

- New pastors often forget to acknowledge the good things a church is already doing. The congrega-tion is a partner with the pastor in ministry and needs to feel affirmed for the gifts that the church brings to that partnership.

- Misunderstanding the motives of the people. Pastors often falsely assume that a small church wants to become a big church. Many people who are attracted to small churches are there because they like the intimacy of a small church. A new pastor must often do the hard work of shaping a congregation's values and desires toward growth and evangelism before sweeping changes can take hold.

- Coming off as angry. Passion for change often is perceived as anger and frustration. My grandfa-ther was visiting on a Sunday when I happened to preach a sermon I considered prophetic, but it was probably just brash and harsh. Afterward he pulled me aside and said, "Remember, Son, you can shear a sheep twice a year, you can roast a sheep once in its lifetime, but you have to feed a sheep every day." I apparently was becoming good at shearing and not so good at feeding.

- Shedding blood and spending political capital on unworthy battles.

- Trying to make changes without building trust.

- Failing to shape the convictions of the congregation. People don't change without first knowing why they ought to be different than they are.

- Failing to adapt to a new context. Too often pastors assume that what worked in one location will translate easily into another. Culture and contexts are always different. Ministry must always be contextual.

- Failing to discern the needs of the congregation and the community. It is an old adage, but people truly will not care how much you know until they know how much you care.

I would encourage readers to study this list carefully. Making the mistakes listed has been fatal to many gifted pastors' ministries. There are ways to bring about change, but in the church change comes slowly, prayerfully, and with a great deal of leadership skill.

To go back to the example of Pastor Ron, there certainly would have been more savvy ways for him to bring about the changes he believed the church needed. He wanted to reduce the size of the board of directors from sixteen to ten. Rather than cashing in all of his social capital in one fell swoop, why not implement this change over time? Pastor Ron could have taken the first year to have the current board and other key laypeople read the reports on why smaller boards are more effective than larger ones. And then after a year of study and dialogue, the board could have moved to reduce its size by two members the first year and by two more each succeeding year until it got down to the desired number. A slower reduction could have likely been accomplished with people wanting to retire or step down naturally. And the gradual change would have significantly lessened the shock for those who would no longer be in leadership. In three to four years the change could have been made with little negative reaction and with little or no damage done to the dynamics of the church leadership system.

Staff changes are never easy. Even staff members who are clearly unsuited for their current positions have people who love and support them. It has been my experience that when a pastoral staff member is released from ministry ungraciously, even people who did not appreciate that person's contributions to ministry become advocates for his or her cause against those in leadership who made the decision. There are varying schools of thought on how to deal with staff transitions. Some leaders I have spoken to and read believe that staff transitions should be made as quickly as possible. I tend to fall on the side of those who advocate for a slower approach. When I come to a new ministry setting where staffing decisions have to be made, I usually take six months to make assessments. And then when the six months are up, if I feel there are changes that need to be made, I will ask the person to stay on for an additional six months and help him or her find a better fit for ministry in another location.

That is not always possible, but I think taking the slower approach is the best method. Remember, people are not hired into ministry. They are called to join the community of the church. Removal of a part of the body must occasionally take place, but it should be done very carefully. There are many ways to deal graciously with staff transitions, but the method Pastor Ron used in my illustration was too sudden, and even with leadership support, pastors rarely are able to recover the social capital that is spent in that kind of hasty move.

Major alterations such as name changes and worship style changes take a great deal of time, grace, and credibility to accomplish. If I were Pastor Ron, I would have put together a special task force, made up of board members and others from the church community, to study the name issue. I would have had them study the question for a minimum of six months and bring a report back to the entire board. I would have held several board meetings and probably a couple of open town hall meetings to discuss the question. This is the kind of decision that seems trivial to a new leader with no history at a church, but to those who have been part of the church for a long time it is always a painful switch. The laity's identity and investment of time and money have been directed toward building up the previous name and reputation of the church. To lose the name is to lose some of that identity.

Especially when the name change includes dropping a denominational marking, passions often seem to run high. It is true that many in the world today are apprehensive about denominationalism and the many, many labels that come with particular denominations. But many other people have committed to a particular church identity on purpose and find great comfort and honor in a particular denominational name. Imagine how most Americans would feel if the president or congress proposed changing the name of the country or announced a plan to alter the design of the flag and its colors. The pastor who receives resistance when trying to make these kinds of changes should not necessarily perceive that resistance as solely a bad thing. People who resist this kind of change do so because they feel deeply invested in and committed to the church. These are not necessarily qualities to fight against. The savvy leader needs instead to find the time and ways to help people share the conviction to change as an expression of their investment and commitment to the church.

The same goes for the worship changes that have been so problematic for churches in the last several decades. You know things are bad when the common way of referring to these transitions is to call them worship wars. (I'm sure God is glorified by our ability to turn worship of him into a source of division in the body.) Those kinds of changes need to be made by moving slowly and bringing the congregation along with the leader. The contributions of people in the past must be honored and celebrated. Again this change could ultimately be accomplished for Pastor Ron with more patience and grace. One of my favorite professors used to remind his students that God has been extremely slow and patient in his redemption of creation and that our patience with the redemption of the local church should be one way for us to reflect the nature of Christ daily in our leadership.

There are crosses worth dying on. I think the most worthy crosses have to do with categories such as justice and mercy. But these crosses are theological and not programmatic. In the first hundred days, do not have a preset strategy for change. Instead, have a hundred-day strategy for loving the people and building up a storehouse of credibility and social capital. You will need that storehouse of favor later when you understand the situation well enough to know what the right changes need to be.

TRANSITION ACCELERATORS

In the business world, leadership experts encourage new leaders to find what they call "transition accelerators."[19] Transition accelerators are those activities that will help a new leader achieve the leadership break-even point, where the net value of the contribution you make to the organization as a new leader is equal to what you now cost the organization. The estimate among CEOs of how long it takes a typical person in management to achieve the break-even point is usually 6.2 months.[20] The purpose of transition accelerators is to help a new leader jump that curve and achieve the break-even point as fast as possible.

Let me suggest five transition accelerators that can help a minister in a new setting accelerate his or her transition: get organized, establish achievable goals, be teachable, begin building a team, and negotiate conflicts.

Get Organized

It may sound trivial, but one of the important ways of accelerating the new pastoral learning curve is by getting things organized from day one. It is much easier to start organized and stay organized than to wait and try to get things organized later on down the road.

Start with your office. Go through whatever old files or materials may be there and determine what is worth keeping and what is not. It might be good for an assistant or someone who has been around the church for a while to give you some advice on what is important and what isn't. You don't want to throw out materials you or the church would later regret losing. If your new church does not have an archive of some kind, it might be good to start one—even if it is only a few filing boxes in an attic or closet. Historical materials are significant, but you don't want your office serving as the archive.

Learn quickly how to use the computer and phone systems that are available. If the church has a Web site, make sure it is updated with your picture and correct contact information as soon as possible. Often in an interim period church Web sites go without updates for months. Learn how to update the Web site or find the person who can make sure all pictures and pertinent information is up-to-date.

Decide what filing systems you are going to use to archive sermon research, letters, and other important church-related business information. Decide how much will be stored digitally and how much will be stored on hard copy. If the church stores data digitally, what data protection steps are in place?

Find out where the important contact numbers and information are located. What is the church's insurance company and who do you contact if there needs to be a claim? What bank does the church work with? If it has debt, what bank holds the debt? What emergency procedures are in place in case of a fire, tornado, or earthquake? Does the church have a volunteer or paid maintenance person for the church, or is there someone else who should be called if a plumbing or electrical problem should develop? Does the church property have an alarm system? If so, how is it turned on and off? Who is called if and when the alarm goes off and what is expected of that person when he or she receives the call? Where are the usual locations and who are the usual counselors called if a person in crisis needs a referral to a mental health professional?

If you are fortunate enough to have an office assistant, quickly establish a good working relationship with him or her and clearly articulate together what the expectations of your working relationship will be. Decide if your assistant will receive all of your calls and emails first, or if people will get direct access to you by phone or email. I have two email addresses and two phone numbers. My primary email account and phone number is published in all church materials and on the church Web site. My assistant has access to those emails and calls, and so I ask her to read those emails and screen those calls before forwarding them on to me. Pastors receive a lot of spam email and a lot of merchandising calls. My assistant is a good filter for what is important and what is not. And during study time or meeting times she serves as a great judge of what situations are important enough to warrant interruptions and which are not. But I also have a private email account and a direct phone line for those people whom I want to have private correspondence and instant accessibility.

If they are not already set up, create notebooks for board and staff meetings that will allow you to keep the agendas and notes from those meetings in one place. Have a new directory printed for your desk so that you will have the numbers and addresses of parishioners handy.

One of the most important ways to get organized is to get your calendar together. Many pastors I speak to try to sketch out a year's worth of sermon ideas and directions. This is made a bit easier if you follow the church year. I have found it helpful to think through the seasons of the year—Advent, Epiphany, Lent, Easter, Pentecost, and then Common Time—when planning out a year's preaching calendar.

As you establish your calendar, decide what days and times your regular meetings will take place. There is probably a traditional time and place already established for meeting with the church's board of directors. Make sure that time works for you and is on your calendar. If you have staff that work for you, establish times for a set weekly meeting. If you have an assistant, it may be good to have a set meeting time at the beginning of the week with him or her so that he or she can keep you aware of upcoming needs and important projects that need your attention.

There are obviously dozens of ways today to keep a calendar. Many people are able to keep them electronically on their computers and smartphones. Thankfully, my computer calendar is now connected not only to my work calendar but to our family calendar at home as well. Before that was the case, I had to make sure my assistant helped me keep my wife informed of evening events I had committed to. I get busy and forgetful and sometimes forget to transfer work dates onto the family calendar. The only feeling worse for me than missing an appointment with someone is springing something on my wife and family at the last minute. With a busy wife, and four kids in sports, keeping all of our calendars synchronized is almost a full-time job of its own.

One of the often overlooked areas in seminary is budgeting. Hopefully, even if you have no training in accounting and business, you are already adept at taking care of your personal finances. If you are not, get help and training immediately. There are many resources available today to help get one's household finances in order. You must do this. Financial problems are the number one cause of struggles in marriage, and they can also devastate a ministry. But if you have learned to be good at financial planning personally, you should be able to make the transition to caring for a church's finances without a whole lot of additional training.

Most churches, even small ones, have a layperson who serves as a treasurer and oversees the ins and outs of the church's accounting needs. If this is not the case, or if you begin to question the integrity or capabilities of the person acting as treasurer, you must try to get some help immediately. Even though you most likely did not receive a lot of financial training in your ministry preparation, once you become pastor, the financial buck stops with you. This is true even if you are a staff pastor. Most staff pastors are given budgets for their ministries, and they are responsible for making sure that those funds are used appropriately and that their budgets are not exceeded.

Learning how the budgeting process is done at the church and learning how to read the budget spreadsheets as soon as possible will accelerate your ability to lead. It is my habit to immediately go back over the previous three years of giving and figure out what the tithing patterns were per quarter during those years. I then use those percentages to calculate what the church needs to receive per week in each quarter in order to stay on track to meet the current budget. I usually print those numbers in the worship folder or bulletin each week so that people can see how much was given last week, how much is needed per week in this quarter of the year, how much has been given for the year, and what the year-to-date giving income should be. I do this so that I can help people know how to give and also so that the church board can have accurate information if decisions need to be made regarding budget cuts at some point during the year.

In most churches reports of some sort must be made to the sponsoring denomination or regional offices. It is important to learn quickly what is required, what is due, who usually sends in that information, and where to get the information necessary for the reports.

There are dozens of other questions you will want to discover in the first hundred days that will help you accelerate your leadership. Are there greeters each week? Who organizes the ushers? Who counts attendance for the service and Sunday school? Are they accurate counters? What is done with that information? What happens to the offering after it is received? What are the methods for counting and what procedures are in place to assure both accuracy and accountability? How are deposits made to the bank? Who makes them and what measures have been put in place to insure safety and accountability? How are the giving records for individuals maintained, and who has access to that information? Is that information kept confidential and are accurate reports given to giving units at the end of the calendar year or at the end of each quarter? Who has keys to the facility and why?

There are lots and lots of issues to get your arms wrapped around. You have time to learn all you need to know, but if you will get organized, set a good calendar, and figure out the week-to-week budget and financial operations of the church, it will greatly accelerate your ability to lead.

Establish Achievable Goals

One of the huge challenges for any new pastor, especially if he or she is coming straight out of college, seminary, or another career, is learning to manage his or her time well. Because a pastor is rarely "on the clock" and there are relatively few set times for a pastor to have to be present, it takes a great deal of self-discipline to structure time productively. It is very easy for pastors to get distracted with trivial things that keep them from accomplishing all they can for the sake of the kingdom. For that reason, I think one way to accelerate leadership is to set daily, weekly, monthly, and yearly achievable goals. I am the kind of person who needs a weekly and daily to-do list to stay focused. It also helps me to outline my study, visitation, personal, facility, and other goals for the month and year.

Many of my pastor friends recommend in the early days of ministry the creation of a monthly pastor's report of activities to distribute to the church board at each monthly meeting. This will help the church leaders know what you have been working on for the past month, which could be important because people often aren't aware of all that goes on in the life of a pastor. But more importantly, many pastors recommend creating this report in the early months and years of ministry as a way of keeping oneself accountable to those in authority for the opportunity to be a minister. Learning to set proper goals and staying motivated will accelerate your ability to move the church forward.

Be Teachable

There are far too many things to know to fulfill well all the roles a pastor can and often does play. No one has the gifts and strengths necessary to run a church of any size all alone. You will need help. But you will also need to discover all you do not know and be open and teachable with others. Church members and leaders are almost always very understanding when a difficult situation arises and you say, "I have no idea how to handle this one. I need help." In my first tenure as a senior pastor I had a standard line I used so often most of the members of the church board could say it with me. I would say, "I am so sorry. They did not cover this in seminary."

I have been in ministry for twenty-five years, nine of them as a senior pastor, and here are just a few things I have faced that I don't remember being covered in my seminary education:

- What do you do when you know a student in your ministry is being abused at home?
- How do you deal with a parent who is upset with you for accusing his or her child of using drugs?
- What do you say to that kid when you have to visit him or her in drug rehabilitation?
- How is the church to deal with the homeless schizophrenic that keeps sleeping on the property and using the church's facilities?

- How do you fix the leaks in a church roof?
- What do you do when a member of the church sues the church?
- How do you deal with a parishioner who makes repeated false claims against a staff member?
- How do you decide which employees to let go of during a financial recession?

The list could go on and on, but these are just a handful of areas where I remember going to people and asking for help. And not just help, but HELP!

It is not only okay but vital to be a continual learner and to have a teachable spirit. The apostle Paul said that God put the various members of the body together for a reason. Not all have the gifts that belong to the eye, nor should they. Every person in the body brings his or her gifts and strengths there for a reason. Accelerate your leadership by being open to receive help from others and being willing to learn.

Begin Building a Team

One important accelerator is a good team. If you are a pastor who will lead a paid staff, you will likely have the advantage of starting with some ministry team in place. As I have mentioned earlier, I would be judicious and deliberate in doing evaluations and making whatever changes are necessary with the pastoral staff.

If you are a staff pastor working with volunteers or a lead pastor with little or no paid pastoral staff, building a good ministry team around you is no less important. Leadership expert Jim Collins argues that one of the leader's first tasks ought to be to ask "who not what." In other words, Collins believes that leaders need to work at gathering the right people around them even before they decide what the task is. Collins remarks about the "good to great" leaders that his study interviewed:

> We expected that good-to-great leaders would begin by setting a new vision and strategy. We found instead that they *first* got the right people on the bus, the wrong people off the bus, and the right people in the right seats—and *then* they figured out where to drive it. The old adage "People are your most important asset" turns out to be wrong. People are *not* your most important asset. The *right* people are.[21]

It does take time to surround yourself, as a pastor, with the right leaders—to get the right people on the bus. But one early step is to recognize what kind of people you will need. Dr. Dick Pritchard, who spent many years as an executive pastor at a large church, and now teaches ministry courses at a Christian university, has told me frequently that he thinks every good ministry team needs three kinds of people: dreamers, doers, and analysts. Pastors by nature tend to be dreamers, but they still need other dreamers who add to their dreams and build upon their larger visions.

But dreamers need doers who will put plans into action. Doers tend to not like meetings because they'd rather be out doing something. A pastor needs lots of doers on their leadership team. They put vision into action.

But leadership teams also need good analysts who will help think through the details and implications of a vision. Analysts can be frustrating at times to both dreamers and doers because to a dreamer they often seem like an obstacle and to a doer they often seem like a source of delay. But every team needs good detail people who analyze the process carefully.

If as a new pastor you will begin on day one to pray for and look for the right dreamers, doers, and analysts who will believe in your leadership and help you move the church forward, it will greatly accelerate your vision.

I would add just a couple pieces of advice about team building—especially during the first hundred days. The first, which I mentioned in chapter 2, is that often the people who appear to be leaders are not, and those who you do not recognize at the beginning (or who are not yet at the church when you arrive) will turn out to be the most significant leaders in the long run. That is obviously not true for everyone. Many who have positions of authority in a church have those positions now because they have a history of providing sound and godly leadership for the church. But often in a transition the people Jesus described as the "shallow soil" and "thorny soil" (see Mark 4) spring up quickly and get energized to participate in a new day of leadership, only to fade away quickly or get choked out by all the other cares and issues in their lives.

Second, in any pastoral transition, at any level, there are people who have been deeply involved in leadership—and often in friendship with the former pastor—who will not make the transition to your team of leaders well. Close friends and key leaders who served the former pastor will often want to immediately assume that same role and friendship with you, only to realize over time that you are very different from, and have a slightly different ministry vision than, the former pastor. Some will come to this conclusion, adjust, and make this transition just fine. But often, the people who worked hardest to be your friends and teammates at the beginning of your tenure will end up being unable to deal with the significant loss their former pastor and friend represents, and they, too, will fade away. Sometimes their leaving can be very painful. It is important you not let that devastate you. There is no way you could replace the former relationship they had with the previous pastor or leader. Those losses are part of the natural ebb and flow of leadership transitions.

It will certainly take more than a hundred days to build the team of leaders you will need to move the church forward. But the sooner you begin to get the right people on the bus and in the right seats, the faster your break-even point will come.

Negotiate Conflict

I hate conflict and so this is one of my least favorite points. But without question a final way to accelerate your move into leadership is to carefully negotiate the conflicts that may exist in the church when you arrive. Robert Ramey puts it this way,

> Maintaining a negative attitude toward conflict will produce only negative experiences with it. Putting a lid on all conflict in the church is difficult, if not impossible—and certainly not desirable. Moreover, avoiding conflict will not make it go away; it will usually build up until it sometimes breaks out with frightening intensity. Would it not be better to learn how to face it and work creatively in the midst of it?[22]

There are at least three reasons for conflict in the church. The first is simply that we are human and we will always have differences of opinion and we will inadvertently hurt one another. In these situations it is critical that you lead by example what it means to turn the other cheek and go the second mile. Lack of conflict is not a mark of the church of Jesus Christ; forgiveness is. And so model—in your ability to deal graciously with criticism and turn wrath away gently—how conflict can be not only handled but also used as a means to strengthen the body of Christ.

Often conflict occurs in the church for a second reason, and that is because people are sinful. A pastor friend and his wife were in a heated argument with a church board member. The issue was relatively trivial, but the argument escalated and became quite intense. Finally, my pastor friend's wife said, "We need to stop this argument right now. I do not think Jesus would be pleased with the nature and direction of this conversation." The board member looked straight at her and said, "I don't care what Jesus would think . . ." and then launched right back into his tirade.

Unfortunately in the church there are times when we all forget to care about what Jesus is thinking about our behavior. Conflicts often happen simply because of our human sin. In those situations as a pastor you have to try and stay calm and not add your sin to the conflict. We pray as a church regularly for God to "forgive us our trespasses as we forgive those who trespass against us." It may be critical for the pastor to model the confession and forgiveness necessary for reconciliation.

But along with being sinful, many people in the church are also sick. There are often forms of brokenness and dysfunction in people's lives that do not excuse their poor behavior but do help a leader to understand them better. I remember as a teenager sitting outside my father's office at church waiting to go home. The only people left at church were my father and I and the couple he was in conflict with behind his closed office door. I could hear the woman, a member of the church, yelling and screaming at my father because her son did not get the kind of score in a church teen talent contest she felt he deserved. That is not the most significant reason for church conflict in history, but it isn't all that unusual either. But what was very unusual was the disproportionate amount of anger coming from her based upon what had happened. It was clear her anger was deeply rooted inside and had little to do with what happened to her son. I only remember that the conversation ended loudly, and it ended this way: The woman shouted at my father, her pastor, "I'll bet you think I need therapy, don't you?" And my father, at his wits end, responded, "More than any person I know."

I don't know if she got the help she needed, but I reflect on that formative experience that night often as a reminder that some conflict is inevitable because, at so many levels, we all are broken and in need of some form of healing. There are chronically broken and damaged people every pastor will have to deal with. In the first hundred days at one of the churches where I was a pastor one of the first conflicts I had to handle was with a church member who had returned after having been removed by the former pastor for saying and doing inappropriate things to the women in the church. He came back when the previous pastor left, hoping for a fresh start. But within weeks he was back into his old habits. His wife defended him, but I had no choice but to create boundaries within which he had to stay for his own protection and the protection of others.

No one enjoys conflict, but it is inevitable even in the early days of a new ministry. Once when I was considering a move—in part to escape some conflicts—a pastor friend reminded me that "in ministry the grass is never greener on the other side. The same problems exist in every church. They just have different first and last names." He was right. But the sooner you can learn to deal with conflict maturely and Christianly, the quicker you will accelerate into the kind of leadership God desires for you as a pastor in his church.

I will remind you again that it takes time to gain credibility and to earn social capital, but if you will get organized, keep yourself motivated by establishing achievable goals, admit what you don't know by remaining teachable, begin to put the right people on the bus in the right places, and strongly but graciously negotiate conflicts, you will help double the leadership value of the first hundred days and reach the break-even point of leadership in record time.

TAKE CARE OF YOURSELF

At this point you may be overwhelmed. So far in the first hundred days I've encouraged you to take care of your family, the sick, the elderly, the church leaders, the youth, the children, and everyone in between. There is one person left to pay careful attention to during the first hundred days of your new ministry—you. You are the temple of the Holy Spirit. You are God's unique creation called to proclaim his good news. Your body is not your own, for you have been bought with a price. This is not an option. You have a divine obligation to take care of yourself.

There are many ways to work at self-care. As I spoke to pastor friends, these were the four encouragements I heard most often: find a mentor, discipline your soul and body care, fight in your own armor, and keep things in their proper perspective.

Find a Mentor

Finding a mentor and friend to walk with you is important throughout a lifetime of ministry, but it is absolutely critical during a pastor's first ministry assignment. I have been blessed through the years to have a family of pastors who have served as mentors. When we have not lived near one another, I have had a phone conversation almost every Sunday night with my mom and dad. We obviously talk about family concerns, but at least 50 percent of those conversations have been working through the issues I am facing in ministry. This book is dedicated to them because I would have failed long ago in ministry without their wise counsel. I was also blessed when I was a staff pastor to have senior pastors who were good role models and mentors. But I continue to be blessed with pastoral colleagues outside the local church and even outside of my denominational circles who serve as important mentors for me.

Every new pastor needs someone outside his or her local church context who can serve as a sounding board and counselor. Farris encourages new pastors after finding a mentor,

> To meet with him or her regularly, at least once each month, particularly in the first year of a new pastorate. The mentor's value is not only in suggesting alternatives and sharing resources, but most essentially in bearing burdens, giving honest feedback, and being unabashedly in the new pastor's corner.[23]

It is not unusual for a pastor's first ministry location to be fairly isolated geographically, and so it might be a challenge to find a pastor mentor nearby. Technology has made it possible for pastors from all around the world to interface with one another daily if desired. It may be a healthy thing to find a group of pastor friends and stay connected via email or some form of social networking. If it is possible to find the resources, it is also recommended that a pastor try and go to one continuing education opportunity or seminar per year. Often the blessing of a seminar is not necessarily the teaching it-self—although that can be valuable—but the fellowship with other pastors around the table and the encourage-ment that takes places there.

Disciplined Soul and Body Care

There was a time when there were as many jokes about pastors and doughnuts as there are about police officers and doughnuts. It seems that things are thank-fully changing. More and more pastors are coming to recognize the need to find disciplined ways to take care of their body and soul.

It is often challenging for a pastor to keep his or her soul healthy. As a pastor I find I am regularly reading the Bible in preparation for the next sermon or the next Bible study class, but I have to work to discipline myself to find time to read the Scripture in order to allow God to speak to me. It's not that sermon and lesson prepa-rations don't nourish my spirit, but it is easy to spend all my time working on what to say to others about God rather than speaking to God, or more importantly, allowing him to speak to me. Some pastors I know discipline themselves to get up early and be with God. Others find a time and place during the day where they can form sacred space and time to be with God. In the first hundred days develop a discipline of soul care.

I would also encourage you to form early disciplines of body care. Sometimes in the church I think that Matt. 18:20 should read, "For where two or three are gathered in my name there I—and a high-calorie casserole—are in the midst of them." The life of the pastor is often filled with lots of food, sedentary meetings, and much stress. That is a recipe for health issues. You must discipline yourself to become or stay active physically.

Work at eating healthy. Set regular patterns of sleep. Take a nap on Sunday afternoon. Always use all of your allotted vacation time. And exercise regularly.

My grandfather was a pastor his entire life and an avid golfer. When he spoke about golf, he would reflect on it in almost sacred terms. I used to tease him that it was not a coincidence for him that the words "God" and "golf" start with the same two letters. He would often say to me, "I love golf because in the midst of stress a fella can go out and take out a lot of his stress on that little white ball." I would giggle and wonder whose face he was visualizing on that Titleist he had teed up.

Some pastors I know own bikes and go cycling a couple of times a week. Some join gyms and try to stick to a regular workout schedule. One of my pastor friends is a swimmer, and he will go out surfing or swimming in the ocean early in the morning. I enjoy running and have tried, with varying degrees of success, to keep a running habit going in order to stay in shape and burn off stress. Whatever activity you find most enjoyable, even if it is just taking a few minutes each day to walk around the block and pray for the neighborhood, start in the early days to develop disciplines of body care that will improve your chances of staying healthy.

Fight in Your Own Armor

In 1 Sam. 17 we are given the great story of David volunteering to face Goliath and Saul trying to put his armor on the young shepherd boy. It did not fit and only made David's quest more ridiculous than it already appeared. This great children's church story always reminds me that each of us must learn to fight in our own armor.

I have tried in this book to give general principles for getting off to a good start that will fit any set of gifts a person might have. But I am sure I have failed at some level. No set of principles, like no suit of armor, can fit the unique strengths of every person. You will have successes and failures that are uniquely yours. And that is okay. Knowing what armor you ought to wear and not wear is a sign of self-awareness and maturity.

One of the most difficult things for a pastor (or a pastor's spouse) to hear any time, but especially in the first hundred days is, "Well, the former pastor used to do . . ." No matter how that sentence ends, it will hurt your feelings. But it does you no good to react to those kinds of comments harshly, and it really does no good to try and deconstruct the gifts of your predecessor. I have found it best to say something like, "You are so right. Thank you for telling me that. Pastor So-and-so was an amazingly gifted leader, and I envy the strengths she had. I don't share all of those same strengths. The gifts God gave me are unique to me. So I apologize if the way

I do things is different than you're used to. Like David, I'm trying to fight in the armor that fits me. Would you be patient with me and keep praying for me that God would use the gifts he's given me to help lead the church forward?"

If that line sounds rehearsed, that is because I have not only rehearsed that line but also used some version of it several times. Early on grow comfortable and secure in the ways God has equipped you to slay the giants in the land where he has placed you. And trust that he has given you the right gifts for this very moment in your church's history.

Finally, Keep Perspective

One of the most important things you can do not only during the first one hundred days but always is to keep a proper perspective on things.

I recently had the privilege in October of 2010 to be a delegate at the Third Lausanne Conference on Global Evangelism in Cape Town, South Africa. It was amazing to gather with over four thousand brothers and sisters in Christ from over two hundred different countries. We

spent eight days worshiping, praying, and strategizing
the future directions of the evangelical church. The conference leaders divided the entire delegation into small
groups by common language, but representing various
world areas. My small group contained church leaders
from Australia, Nigeria, India, Malaysia, and Lebanon. It
was amazing to hear their stories of God's blessing, but
also for several of my new friends, it was awe-inspiring
to hear the stories of God's sustaining power during
persecution.

One of the morning sessions was devoted to the idea
of breaking down walls between groups of people and
forming new patterns of reconciliation. After several
speakers shared their dramatic stories from places like
Rwanda and North Korea, they asked us to share around
our tables about how God is breaking down barriers
in our own settings. The people around my table each
shared amazing stories of God's reconciliation. The
Malaysian, the Lebanese, and the Nigerian each shared
harrowing stories of restored relationship following peri-
ods of great violence between Muslims and Christians in
their communities. The woman from India is a human

rights lawyer who shared terrifying and heartbreaking stories about the work she is doing among the Dalits or "untouchables"—those who are part of the lowest caste in India.

Finally they came to me and asked, "Scott, how is God breaking down barriers and bringing about reconciliation where you are?" Looking back I could have shared some of the great ways God is helping us to form a multicultural, multigenerational, and diverse economic congregation, but all I could think to say at the time was, "Well, God is helping us to break down the walls between those who prefer contemporary worship and those who prefer traditional." In comparison to their heroic stories, what I was about to say sounded so inane that I thankfully kept my mouth shut and just asked if I could pass on this particular subject.

Hearing the stories of the trials faced by brothers and sisters around the world in some of the most challenging places on the planet as they continue to work proclaiming the gospel helped me gain a much-needed perspective on the significance (or apparent lack thereof) of my own challenges.

I would encourage you, in the end, to keep a healthy perspective on your ministry. Getting off to a good start in the first hundred days is important, but the One who raised Jesus from the dead can redeem your ministry even if you get off to a difficult start. Remember what you learned as a child: You "are weak, but He is strong."[24] God called you to proclaim his message, but he is the One who saves. The ministry is yours (on loan), but the church is the Lord's.

Do everything you can to let the Spirit lead you and help you to set the right trajectory in the first hundred days. "The one who calls you is faithful, and he will continue to be faithful" (1 Thess. 5:24, ISV).

EPILOGUE
IF ALL ELSE FAILS . . .

I hope this book has been helpful and has given
you some practical ideas for getting your new ministry
position started in the right direction. It isn't impossible
to recover from a bad start. Both the apostles Peter and
Paul teach us that. But I am convinced that most great
endings can be traced back to very good beginnings.

I would like to leave you with two final thoughts.

Most of what I have written in the previous chapters
has been an attempt to be as pragmatic as possible. I
have tried to take the best of what I have learned from
pastors and other organizational leaders and made their
advice as practical as possible. But those of us who are
pastors should never forget that in the end our leadership is not primarily organizational but spiritual. In the
beginning, middle, and end we have to be intimately
connected to the Father, through Christ, and to the leading of his Holy Spirit. Even the most spiritually attuned
leader can be undone by poor leadership practices, but

the greatest organizational guru will lead the church nowhere if he or she does not develop the ears to hear what the Spirit is saying to the church.

One of my favorite ancient "desert fathers" is Abbot Joseph. There is a well known story about Joseph that goes like this:

> There came to the abbot Joseph the abbot Lot, and said to him, "Father, according to my strength I keep a modest rule of prayer and fasting and meditation and quiet, and according to my strength I purge my imagination: what more must I do?" The old man, rising, held up his hands against the sky, and his fingers became like ten torches of fire, and he said, "If thou wilt, thou shalt be made wholly flame."[25]

So if all else fails, by the power of the Spirit, light yourself on fire. People want to follow leaders who love God with all of the heart, soul, mind, and strength and are working at loving their neighbors as themselves. Without a sustaining vision a community is set adrift. And so have a passion for the Lord and stay plugged into the leading of God's Spirit.

Finally, be committed to the right results. I recently heard Pastor Jack Hayford—the longtime pastor of the very large Church on the Way in Van Nuys, California—remark that whenever he is asked how he built Church on the Way into a megachurch he replies, "It was never my intent to build a big church. The calling God gave me was to help him to build 'big people' for his kingdom. Having a big church was simply the outgrowth of God building big people."

I love that statement. There is a lot of pressure on pastors to lead ministries that grow—and that grow quickly. One of the primary reasons pastors get off to bad starts is because the pressure to grow gets in the way of the calling to love and to serve. So as you get your ministry aligned, don't forget that the ultimate goal is not to grow a big church but to lead people to become great citizens in God's kingdom.

May God grant you his wisdom and his peace as you follow his calling—not just in the first hundred days of your ministry—but in all the great days to come.

NOTES

1. A nautical term from the days of sailing ships when new recruits had to learn how to tie knots and which rope hauled up which sail. After which they would "know the ropes."

2. William Bridges, *Managing Transitions: Making the Most of Change* (Reading, Mass.: Addison-Wesley, 1991), 3.

3. From the introduction.

4. Plato, *The Apology of Socrates* (London: Robinson and Co., 1901), 77.

5. Richard Alan Krieger, *Civilization's Quotations: Life's Ideal* (Washington, D.C.: Algora Publishing, 2002), 160.

6. Plato, *The Dialogues of Plato* (New York: Scribner, Armstrong, and Co., 1873), 1:20.

7. For information on the StrengthsQuest materials, go to www.strengthsquest.com or see Tom Rath, *StrengthsFinder 2.0* (New York: Gallup Press, 2007); Tom Rath and Barry Conchie, *Strengths-Based Leadership: Great Leaders, Teams, and Why People Follow* (New York: Gallup Press, 2009); or Albert L. Winseman, Donald O. Clifton, and Curt Liesveld, *Living Your Strengths: Discover Your God-Given Talents and Inspire Your Community* (New York: Gallup Press, 2004).

8. This great illustration comes from Angie Best-Boss, *Surviving Your First Year as Pastor: What Seminary Couldn't Teach You* (Valley Forge, Pa.: Judson Press, 1999), xi-xii.

9. John T. Galloway, *Ministry Loves Company: A Survival Guide for Pastors* (Louisville, Ky.: Westminster John Knox Press, 2003), 10.

10. See T. Scott Daniels, *Seven Deadly Spirits: The Message of Revelation's Letters for Today's Church* (Grand Rapids: Baker Academic, 2009), 17.

11. Lawrence W. Farris, *Ten Commandments for Pastors New to a Congregation* (Grand Rapids: Eerdmans, 2003), 7.

12. See Robert H. Ramey Jr., *The Pastor's Start-Up Manual: Beginning a New Pastorate* (Nashville: Abingdon Press, 1995), 54.

13. Ibid., 18.

14. Roy W. Oswald, *New Beginnings: A Pastorate Start Up Workbook* (Chicago: The Alban Institute, 1989), 1-2.

15. See Ramey, *Pastor's Start-Up Manual,* 97-98.

16. Farris, *Ten Commandments for Pastors,* 24.

17. Michael Watkins, *The First Ninety Days: Critical Success Strategies for Leaders at All Levels* (Boston: Harvard Business School Press, 2003), 80.

18. See Patrick Lencioni, *Death by Meeting: A Leadership Fable About Solving the Most Painful Problem in Business* (San Francisco: Jossey-Bass, 2004), 226-32.

19. See Watkins, *First Ninety Days,* 2.

20. Ibid.

21. Jim Collins, *Good to Great: Why Some Companies Make the Leap . . . and Others Don't* (New York: Harper Business, 2001), 13.

22. Ramey, *Pastor's Start-Up Manual,* 59.

23. Farris, *Ten Commandments for Pastors,* 93.

24. Anna B. Warner, "Jesus Loves Me" (1860), Cyber Hymnal, http://www.hymntime.com/tch/htm/j/e/s/jesuslme.htm.

25. Helen Waddell, *The Desert Fathers* (Ann Arbor, Mich.: Ann Arbor Paperback, 1957), 112.

"... a spell-binding demonstration of how metaphor, imagery, and verbal cinematography can be used to reach the 21st-century mind."

—*Dr. Darrell Moore, Nazarene Theological Seminary*

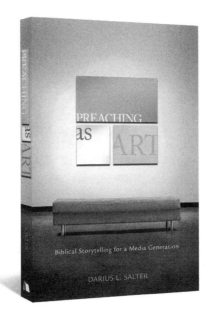

This book shows preachers how to use the Bible's colorful imagery and literary brilliance to celebrate God's amazing story. Darius Salter conveys practical ideas, illustrations, and a variety of media options to help pastors transform their messages into art forms that invite listeners to experience Scripture and encounter God as never before.

PREACHING AS ART
Biblical Storytelling for a Media Generation
By Darius L. Salter
ISBN 978-0-8341-2359-5

 BEACON HILL PRESS
OF KANSAS CITY

Available online and wherever books are sold.

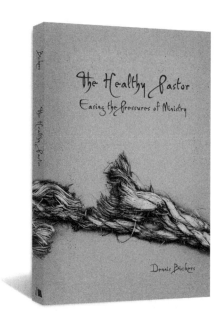

The Healthy Pastor seeks to provide insights into the expectations churches and ministers have of the pastor's role. Dennis Bickers addresses some of the common pressure points every minister experiences and provides solutions to those pressures. Ministers will be challenged to create balance in several areas of their lives: their relationship with God, family, the church, their self, and—for bivocational ministers—their second job.

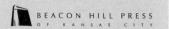